The Four Pillars of Freedom

Your Complete Life Transformation Guide

CHANDAN BERA

Personal Message from Chandan Bera

I'm writing this book because I have felt stuck in life —more than once. I've experienced the frustration of knowing I was capable of more, but not knowing how to break free from the invisible chains holding me back. Whether it was financial stress, confusion about my purpose, struggling with relationships, or simply feeling lost — I've been there.

Through years of learning, experimenting, and seeking guidance from some of the world's best mentors —Robin Sharma, Jim Rohn, Brian Tracy, and many others— I discovered that success and freedom are not accidents. They are the result of clear systems, consistent action, and the right mindset.

This book is my humble attempt to share everything I've learned, in a simple, practical way — so that no matter where you are today, you can build a life of freedom, success, and true happiness.

This book is not just theory. It's filled with real-life exercises, proven strategies, and lessons from people who've turned their struggles into success. If you feel stuck, this book is for you. Let's walk this path together.

— Chandan Bera

Contents

CONTENTS

1. Why You Feel Stuck & How to Break Free

1.1 Introduction – The Truth About Feeling Stuck

Have you ever felt like you're trapped in the same cycle, unable to move forward no matter how hard you try? You wake up every morning with a long to-do list, but at the end of the day, it feels like nothing significant has changed. You might have dreams of financial independence, a fulfilling career, or better relationships, yet you find yourself stuck in the same place year after year. If this sounds familiar, you're not alone.

Feeling stuck is one of the most frustrating experiences in life. It makes you question your potential, doubt your abilities, and sometimes even lose hope in the future. But here's the good news: **being stuck is not a permanent state.** It's simply a phase—one that you can break free from with the right mindset and actions. This book is designed to help you do just that.

Before we dive into strategies for breaking free, let's explore why so many people feel trapped in life. Understanding the root causes will help you recognize your own patterns and take meaningful action.

1. The Real Reasons You Feel Stuck

a) Fear of Change

Change is scary. Our brains are wired to prefer comfort and familiarity, even when those conditions aren't serving us. You might be in a job you hate, but the fear of financial instability keeps you from looking for something better. You might be in an unfulfilling relationship, but the thought of being alone makes you stay. Fear of the unknown keeps you in the someplace, even when you know you deserve better.

b) Lack of Clear Goals

Many people feel stuck because they don't have a clear vision of where they want to go. If you don't know your destination, how can you take steps toward it? Without well-defined goals, life becomes a series of random events rather than a journey with purpose.

c) Negative Self-Talk and Limiting Beliefs

"I'm not good enough." "I don't have the skills." "Success is for others, not for me." These negative thoughts create invisible barriers that prevent you from moving forward. The most successful people in the world have one thing in common—they believe in their ability to grow, learn, and achieve.

d) Waiting for the "Perfect" Time

One of the biggest reasons people stay stuck is because they wait for the perfect moment to start. They tell themselves, "I'll start a business when I have more money," or "I'll focus on my health after this busy period." The truth is, **there is no perfect time.** The best time to start is always now.

e) Lack of a Support System

Success doesn't happen in isolation. If you are surrounded by people who discourage you or don't support your growth, it becomes much harder to break free from stagnation. Your environment plays a significant role in shaping your mindset and actions.

2. The First Steps to Breaking Free

Step 1: Accept That Feeling Stuck Is Normal

The first step to overcoming any challenge is to accept it. Feeling stuck doesn't mean you're a failure—it means you're human. Many successful people have experienced this phase before their breakthroughs. Instead of resisting or feeling frustrated, embrace it as an opportunity to grow.

Step 2: Identify What's Holding You Back

Take some time to reflect on what's keeping you stuck. Is it fear? A lack of clarity? Negative self-talk? Write down your thoughts in a journal. Once you identify the barriers, you can start working on solutions.

Exercise: Identifying Your Barriers

Take a piece of paper and draw a line down the middle. On the left side, write "What's keeping me stuck?" List all the reasons, fears, and obstacles you can think of. On the right side, write "What would freedom look like? "Describe your ideal life if none of these barriers existed. This exercise helps you clearly see both what's holding you back and what you're working toward.

Step 3: Define Your Goals Clearly

A clear vision gives you direction. Instead of saying, "I want to be successful," be specific. Define what success means to you. Is it earning a certain amount of money? Finding work you love? Improving your health? The more specific you are, the easier it becomes to create a plan.

Step 4: Take Small, Consistent Actions

You don't need to change your life overnight. Small, consistent steps lead to massive transformation over time. If you want to improve your health, start by walking for 10 minutes a day. If you want financial freedom, start by saving a small percentage of your income. Progress is more important than perfection.

Step 5: Surround Yourself with the Right People Jim Rohn famously said, "You are the average of the five people you spend the most time with." If your environment is keeping you stuck, change it. Find mentors, join communities, and surround yourself with people who inspire and challenge you.

3. Understanding the Four Pillars of a Fulfilled Life

Success and freedom are built on four pillars:

Health, Wealth, Relationships, and Purpose. If any of these areas are neglected, life feels incomplete. In the upcoming chapters, we will dive deep into each of these pillars and explore actionable strategies to improve them.

a) Health – Your Foundation for Success Your energy levels, mental clarity, and emotional stability depend on your health. Without a strong body and mind, achieving success in other areas becomes difficult.

b) Wealth – Achieving Financial Freedom Money isn't everything, but financial stress can keep you trapped. Learning how to manage, grow, and multiply your income gives you the freedom to live on your own terms.

c) Relationships – The Key to Happiness

No matter how successful you become, life feels empty without meaningful relationships. Building strong personal and professional connections is essential for a fulfilling life.

d) Purpose – Finding Meaning in Your Work and Life

Having a sense of purpose makes every challenge worthwhile. When you align your career and daily actions with your purpose, life becomes more rewarding.

4. Your Action Plan: Breaking Free from Feeling Stuck

Write Down What's Holding You Back – Identify your fears, limiting beliefs, and excuses.

Set a Clear Goal – Choose one area of life (health, wealth, relationships, or purpose) and define a clear goal.

Take One Small Action Today – Don't wait for the perfect time. Start with something small and manageable.

Find a Mentor or Role Model – Learn from people who have already achieved what you want.

Change Your Daily Habits – Success comes from daily habits, not one-time actions. Identify and build positive habits.

Journal Prompt

What is one small step you can take today to move toward the life you want? It doesn't have to be perfect or significant—just a small action that breaks the pattern of staying stuck.

Final Thoughts

Feeling stuck is temporary. It's a sign that you are ready for change. The difference between people who stay stuck and those who break free is action. The moment you decide to take control of your life, everything starts to shift.

In the next chapters, we will explore each pillar of success in detail, starting with **Health – Your Foundation for Success**. Get ready to transform your life!

1.2 What Real Freedom & Success Mean

What comes to mind when you think of freedom and success? For many, the image of a luxury car, a large house, or financial wealth immediately appears. While these material possessions can be part of success, true freedom and success go far beyond what you own or how much money you have in your bank account.

In this chapter, we'll explore what real freedom and success mean—not according to society's standards, but according to what truly fulfils you and creates a life of meaning, purpose, and joy.

The Illusion of Success

Success as portrayed in media often focuses on external achievements: prestigious job titles, expensive possessions, social recognition, and wealth accumulation. While these accomplishments might bring temporary satisfaction, they rarely lead to lasting fulfilment.

Consider the stories of highly "successful" people who, despite having everything society values, still feel empty, stressed, or unfulfilled. Some celebrities, business tycoons, and high-achievers openly admit to struggling with anxiety, depression, or a sense of meaninglessness despite their external success.

This paradox exists because we've been conditioned to chase aversion of success that doesn't necessarily align with our core values, natural talents, or authentic desires. True success isn't about ticking boxes on a standardized list—it's about creating life that resonates with your deepest self.

Redefining Success: The Four Dimensions

Authentic success encompasses four key dimensions:

1. **Internal Success** – The quality of your relationship with yourself. This includes self-awareness, self-acceptance, confidence, peace of mind, and emotional well-being. Without internal success, external achievements feel hollow.

2. External Success – The conventional markers of achievement, including career progression, financial stability, material comfort, and recognition for your work. While not

the complete picture, external success provides resources and opportunities that can enhance other aspects of life.

3. Relational Success – The depth and quality of your connections with others. This involves maintaining nurturing relationships, building a supportive community, and contributing positively to others' lives. Even with internal and external success, life feels empty without meaningful connections.

4. Transcendent Success – Your contribution to something greater than yourself. This might involve spiritual growth, leaving a positive legacy, or making a difference in causes you care about. Transcendent success gives meaning to all other forms of achievement.

Exercise: Your Success Inventory

Rate yourself from 1-10 in each dimension of success:

Internal Success (1-10): _________

External Success (1-10): _________

Relational Success (1-10): _________

Transcendent Success (1-10): _________

Where are you thriving? Where could you use more balance? What dimension, if improved, would most enhance your overall sense of fulfilment?

True Freedom Defined

Like success, freedom is often misunderstood. Many associate freedom solely with the absence of restrictions: no boss, no schedule, no responsibilities. However, this narrow definition fails to capture what true freedom entails.

Authentic freedom consists of:

1. Financial Freedom – Not just being rich, but having enough resources to live without constant financial stress. It means having choices about how you spend your time without being solely driven by monetary need.

2. Time Freedom – The ability to allocate your time according to your priorities rather than external demands. This doesn't mean having nothing to do; it means having greater control over what you do with your time.

3. Emotional Freedom – Liberation from destructive emotional patterns, including excessive worry, regret, resentment, and fear. Emotional freedom means responding to life's challenges from a place of clarity rather than reactivity.

4. Mental Freedom – Freedom from limiting beliefs, societal conditioning, and negative thought patterns that keep you trapped. Mental freedom allows you to think independently and make choices based on your authentic values rather than external pressures.

5. Physical Freedom – Having the health, energy, and vitality to pursue your goals and enjoy your life. Without physical freedom, other forms of freedom become difficult to enjoy fully.

6. Social Freedom – The ability to create and maintain relationships that nurture and support you rather than drainer constrain you. It includes the freedom to be authentically yourself in your interactions.

7. Spiritual/Purpose Freedom – The liberty to pursue what gives your life meaning and purpose. This might involve religious practice, creative expression, service to others, or any path that connects you to something greater than yourself.

The Paradox of Freedom

Here's a truth that might seem contradictory at first: **Real freedom doesn't come from an absence of commitment but from the right commitments.** When you commit to values, relationships, and purposes that align with your authentic self, these commitments don't constrain you—they liberate you.

Think about it: The disciplined athlete has more physical freedom than someone who never exercises. The person who commits to developing their talents has more creative freedom than someone who never practices. The individual who builds deep relationships has more emotional freedom than someone who avoids connection.

> "Freedom is not the absence of commitments, but the ability to
>
> choose—and commit myself to—what is best for me." —
>
> Paulo Coelho

Success and Freedom: An Integrated Approach

When properly understood, success and freedom aren't separate pursuits—they're interconnected facets of a well-lived life. True success creates greater freedom, and genuine freedom enables deeper success.

Consider how this integration works across the four life pillars:

Health: When you succeed in building robust physical and mental health, you gain the freedom to pursue activities with energy and focus. Conversely, the freedom to make health-supporting choices leads to greater success in physical well-being.

Wealth: Success in creating financial stability gives you the freedom to make choices based on values rather than necessity. And the freedom to pursue work aligned with your strengths enables greater financial success over time.

Relationships: Successful relationships free you from isolation and create a support network for all life's endeavours. The freedom to be authentic in relationships leads to deeper, more fulfilling connections.

Purpose: Success in discovering and expressing your purpose provides the ultimate freedom—living a life of meaning. Freedom from societal expectations allows you to define and pursue success on your own terms.

Journal Prompt

What would true freedom look like in your life? Not based on social media images or others' expectations, but what would make YOU feel truly free? Write without filtering or judging your answers.

Creating Your Personal Definition of Success

It's time to create your own definition of success—one that resonates with your values, strengths, and deepest desires. This definition will serve as your compass throughout the journey ahead.

To create this personal definition, consider these questions:

When you're 80 years old, looking back on your life, what would make you feel you've lived successfully?

What activities make you lose track of time because you're so engaged?

What achievements would give you a sense of pride, regardless of whether anyone else noticed them?

What qualities or values do you most admire in others?

If you had six months to live, what would become most important to you?

Use your answers to craft a personal success statement. Don't worry about making it perfect—this is a living document that will evolve as you grow.

Exercise: Your Personal Success Statement

Complete this sentence: "To me, living successfully means..."

Make your statement as specific and authentic as possible. Include elements from each dimension of success—internal, external, relational, and transcendent.

Breaking Free from Others' Definitions

One of the greatest obstacles to authentic success is allowing others to define it for you. Whether it's parents, peers, media, or cultural norms, external definitions of success can pull you away from your true path.

Here are some signs you might be chasing someone else's version of success:

You feel accomplished but not fulfilled

You can't explain why certain goals matter to you, just that they should

You feel more relief than joy when you achieve something

You rarely feel present and engaged in your daily activities

You're more concerned with how your life looks than how it feels

To break free from others' definitions, practice these strategies:

Mindful Questioning: Before pursuing a goal, ask, "Is this truly important to ME, or am I doing this to impress or please others?"

Value Alignment: Ensure your pursuits align with your core values rather than external pressures.

Regular Reflection: Schedule time to assess whether your current path feels right for you, not just what looks successful to others.

Curiosity About Alternate Paths: Explore different ways of living and working before committing to conventional routes.

Freedom and Success as a Journey, Not a Destination

Perhaps the most important realization about freedom and success is that they're not fixed destinations you arrive at once and for all. They're ongoing experiences that deepen and evolve throughout life.

This journey-oriented perspective offers several advantages:

It relieves perfectionist pressure: You don't have to "get it right" all at once.

It encourages experimentation: Different seasons of life might call for different expressions of success.

It promotes presence: Instead of always looking toward a future achievement, you can experience success and freedom in the present moment.

It focuses on growth rather than comparison: Success becomes about your personal evolution rather than measuring up to others.

"Success is not a destination, but the road that you're on. Being successful means that you 'reworking hard and walking your walk every day."— Marlon Wayans

Case Study: Redefining Success

Maya was a high-achieving corporate lawyer who, by conventional standards, had "made it." She had a six-figure salary, recognition in her field, and all the material trappings of success. Yet she felt exhausted, disconnected, and empty. After a health scare at age 38, Maya began questioning her definition of success. Through careful reflection, she realized that her authentic values cantered around creativity, connection, and contribution—none of which were being fulfilled in her current life.

Over the next two years, Maya gradually transformed her life. She reduced her work hours, started a small creative consultancy helping nonprofits, deepened her relationships, and prioritized her health. Her income decreased, but her sense of time freedom, emotional wellbeing, and purpose increased dramatically.

To outsiders, it might have looked like Maya was becoming "less successful." But according to her recalibrated definition—one that balanced internal, external, relational, and transcendent dimensions—she was finally experiencing true success.

Conclusion

Real freedom and success aren't measured by bank accounts, job titles, or social media likes. They're measured by how aligned your life is with your authentic self, how much peace you experience amid life's challenges, the quality of your relationships, and your contribution to causes greater than yourself.

As we continue through this book, keep refining your personal definitions of freedom and success. Let them guide your choices and evaluations rather than defaulting to external standards. In the next chapter, we'll explore the critical process of self-discovery—understanding who you are and what you truly want—which forms the foundation for authentic success and freedom.

1.3 Self-Discovery: Knowing Who You Are & What You Want

Have you ever been so busy climbing the ladder of success that you forgot to check whether it was leaning against the right wall? Many people spend decades pursuing goals that don't truly reflect who they are or what they want, only to realize later that they've been building someone else's dream.

This chapter focuses on perhaps the most crucial element of breaking free: self-discovery. Before you can create a life of freedom and success, you need to understand who you really are and what you genuinely want.

The Self-Discovery Crisis

We're living in an age of identity confusion. With constant exposure to others' lives through social media, endless career options, and rapidly changing social norms, many people struggle to develop a clear sense of self. This lack of self-knowledge creates several problems:

Making decisions becomes difficult because you don't know what you truly value

You're more susceptible to others' influence and validation

You might achieve external goals but still feel empty inside

Relationships suffer because you can't authentically connect when you're disconnected from yourself

Energy gets wasted on pursuits that don't align with your true nature

Self-discovery isn't a luxury—it's a necessity for creating a life that feels genuinely successful and free.

The Three Dimensions of Self-Discovery

Comprehensive self-discovery involves exploring three interconnected dimensions:

1.Self-Awareness: Understanding your personality, strengths, weaknesses, values, and patterns. This is about seeing yourself clearly—both your gifts and your blind spots.

2. Self-Acceptance: Embracing your entire self—including the parts you might wish were different. Without self-acceptance, you'll waste energy fighting against your nature rather than working with it.

3. Self-Alignment: Making choices that honour your authentic self rather than conforming to external expectations. This is where awareness and acceptance translate into action.

Let's explore practical approaches to developing each dimension.

Self-Awareness: Seeing Yourself Clearly

Self-awareness begins with curiosity about who you really are beneath social conditioning, habitual patterns, and the roles you play. Here are several pathways to deeper self-awareness:

Identify Your Core Values

Your values are the principles that matter most to you—freedom, family, creativity, achievement, wisdom, etc. When your life aligns with your values, you feel fulfilled. When it conflicts with them, you feel tension.

Exercise: Value Discovery

1. From the list below, circle the 10 values that resonatemost with you:

Achievement, Adventure, Authenticity, Balance, Beauty, Community, Compassion, Courage, Creativity, Curiosity, Determination, Fairness, Faith, Family, Freedom, Friendship, Growth, Happiness, Harmony, Health, Honesty, Humor, Independence, Innovation, Integrity, Justice, Kindness, Knowledge, Leadership, Learning, Love, Loyalty, Mindfulness, Openness, Optimism, Passion, Peace, Pleasure, Power, Recognition, Respect, Responsibility, Security, Service, Simplicity, Spirituality, Stability, Success, Tradition, Truth, Wealth, Wisdom

2. Narrow your selection to the top 5 that feel most essential to you.

3. Rank these 5 in order of importance.

4. For each value, write what it means to you personally and how it might guide your choices.

Discover Your Natural Strengths

Your innate strengths are activities and ways of thinking that energize you and come naturally. Unlike skills (which can be developed regardless of natural inclination), strengths represent your inherent talents and preferences.

To identify your strengths:

Reflect on activities where you lose track of time because you're so engaged

Consider what others consistently praise or come to you for

Notice what types of problems you solve easily while others struggle

Think about what you've always been drawn to, even as a child

Several assessment tools can help identify your strengths, including Gallup StrengthsFinder, VIA Character Strengths Survey, and the Clifton Strengths assessment. These provide language and frameworks to understand your natural gifts.

Clarify Your Personality Patterns

Your personality influences how you process information, make decisions, manage energy, and interact with others. Understanding these patterns helps you create environments and routines that work with—rather than against—your nature.

While no personality framework captures your full complexity, models like the Myers-Briggs Type Indicator, Enneagram, and Big Five can provide useful insights about your tendencies and preferences.

Recognize Your Emotional Patterns

Your emotional landscape offers crucial information about what matters to you. Regular emotional awareness practices help you recognize patterns and triggers that influence your choices.

Journal Prompt: Emotional Mapping

For one week, at the end of each day, answer these questions:

1. What brought me joy or energy today?

2. What drained me or caused stress?

3. What patterns do I notice across different situations?

4. What does this tell me about what matters to me?

Self-Acceptance: Embracing Your Whole Self

Self-awareness without self-acceptance can actually increase suffering. If you see yourself clearly but continually reject what you see, you'll remain trapped in self-judgment and resistance.

Self-acceptance doesn't mean abandoning growth—it means starting from a place of fundamental worthiness rather than deficiency. From this foundation, development becomes an expression of self-love rather than self-rejection.

Practices that foster self-acceptance include:

Distinguish Between Voice of Judgment and Voice of Discernment

The voice of judgment says, "I'm not good enough" or "I should be different." It's harsh, absolute, and focuses on your worth as a person.

The voice of discernment says, "This approach isn't working well" or "I'd like to develop in this area." It's objective, specific, and focuses on behaviours rather than your worth.

Learning to recognize and question the voice of judgment while listening to the voice of discernment is crucial for self-acceptance.

Practice Self-Compassion

Research by Dr. Kristin Neff shows that self-compassion—treating yourself with the same kindness you would offer a good friend—leads to greater emotional resilience, motivation, and relationship satisfaction than self-criticism.

Self-compassion involves three elements:

Mindfulness: Observing your thoughts and feelings without over-identifying with them

Common humanity: Recognizing that struggle and imperfection are part of shared human experience

Self-kindness: Offering yourself understanding rather than harsh judgment

Exercise: Self-Compassion Letter

Think of an area where you tend to be self-critical. Write a letter to yourself from the perspective of an unconditionally loving friend who sees all your strengths and struggles. What would this compassionate friend say about your situation? How would they encourage you?

Embrace Your Shadow Side

The "shadow" represents aspects of yourself that you've rejected, denied, or disowned—often because they didn't fit with how you wanted to see yourself or how others wanted you to be.

Ironically, rejecting parts of yourself doesn't eliminate them—it pushes them into unconscious expression, often in ways that sabotage your conscious goals. Acknowledging and integrating your shadow aspects brings greater wholeness and authenticity.

Signs of shadow aspects might include:

Traits you strongly dislike in others (often projections of disowned parts of yourself)

Behaviours that seem to happen "despite" your intentions

Recurring patterns that you can't seem to break

Areas where your stated values and actual behaviours consistently conflict

Self-Alignment: Living Authentically

Self-awareness and self-acceptance lay the groundwork for the third dimension of self-discovery: self-alignment. This means designing your life to reflect who you truly are rather than who you think you should be.

Areas where alignment creates freedom and fulfilment include:

Aligned Work

Work consumes a significant portion of your time and energy. When it aligns with your values, strengths, and personality, it becomes a source of fulfilment rather than merely Apa check.

Ask yourself:

Does my work allow me to express my core values?

Does it utilize my natural strengths?

Is the environment compatible with my personality?

Does it contribute to something I find meaningful?

If you answered "no" to most of these questions, you may need to consider ways to bring greater alignment—whether through changing roles, workplaces, careers, or starting your own venture.

Aligned Relationships Authentic connection requires showing up as your true self rather than who you think others want you to be. This vulnerability may feel risky, but it's the only path to genuine intimacy and belonging.

Signs of misalignment in relationships include:

Feeling exhausted after social interactions

Continuously censoring your thoughts and feelings. Losing your sense of self in relationships. Maintaining connections out of obligation rather than genuine desire. Creating aligned relationships might involve setting clearer boundaries, expressing your authentic needs and feelings, or in some cases, transitioning away from relationships that require you to diminish your true self.

Aligned Environment

Your physical surroundings and daily structure either supporter hinder your authentic expression. An introvert might need quiet spaces for reflection, while an extravert might thrive in collaborative environments. A person who values creativity might need visual stimulation, while someone who values order might need minimalist organization. Consider how you can adjust your environment to support your authentic needs and preferences, rather than fighting against them.

Exercise: Alignment Audit

For each area below, rate how aligned it feels with your authentic self (1 = completely misaligned, 10 = perfectly aligned):

Career/Work: _________

Daily Routine: _________

Home Environment: _________

Close Relationships: _________

Social Circle: _________

Expression/Creativity: ________

Physical Health Habits: ________

For areas scoring below 6, identify one small step you could take to bring greater alignment.

What Do You Really Want?

With greater self-awareness, self-acceptance, and a commitment to alignment, you're ready to tackle the fundamental question: What do you really want?

Many people struggle to answer this question because:

They've spent more time focusing on what others want for them

They fear disappointment if they acknowledge their true desires

They've disconnected from their internal guidance system

They confuse surface wants (status symbols, external validation) with deeper desires (meaningful contribution, authentic connection)

To reconnect with your authentic desires:

Distinguish Between "Should Wants" and "True Wants"

"Should wants" come from external expectations, social conditioning, and the desire to impress others. They often feel heavy, anxiety-producing, and driven by fear of inadequacy.

"True wants" arise from your authentic self. They feel energizing, resonant, and connected to meaning and purpose, even when challenging.

When considering any goal or desire, ask: "If no one would ever know about this achievement, would I still want it?"

Explore Multiple Possibilities

Instead of pressuring yourself to identify one perfect path, explore multiple possibilities that might express your authentic self. The design thinking concept of "prototyping"

applies here—trying small experiments to test different directions before committing fully.

Journal Prompt: Multiple Futures

Imagine three different possible futures for yourself, all of which could be fulfilling in different ways. Describe each in detail—where you live, what work you do, who you spend time with, how you contribute. Notice which elements across these different scenarios create the most sense of rightness and energy.

Listen to Your Body

Your body often knows what you want before your conscious mind does. It responds with energy, openness, and relaxation to options aligned with your authentic desires and with tension, constriction, or fatigue to misaligned paths.

Practice checking in with physical sensations when considering different choices. Does one option create a sense of expansion in your chest while another creates tightness? These bodily signals provide valuable guidance about your true desires.

The Continuous Journey of Self-Discovery

Self-discovery isn't a one-time event but a lifelong process. As you grow and evolve, new aspects of your authentic self-emerge. The person you are at 35 has different insights and desires than the person you were at 25—and the person you'll be at 50 will have yet another perspective.

Rather than trying to "solve" yourself once and for all, commit to ongoing curiosity and exploration. Regular reflection practices keep you connected to your evolving authentic self:

Annual personal retreats to review and realign

Weekly reflection on what felt energizing versus depleting

Daily check-ins with your body and emotions

Periodic "life experiments" to test new directions

Case Study: Alex's Self-Discovery Journey

Alex had always been "the responsible one"—pursuing a stable career in finance, buying a house at 28, and doing everything according to plan. On paper, his life was successful, but he felt increasingly disconnected and restless.

Through a structured self-discovery process, Alex realized several important truths:

- His core values included creativity, freedom, and adventure—none of which were expressed in his current life

- His natural strengths involved connecting ideas across different fields and communicating complex concepts simply

- His personality thrived on variety and new challenges rather than predictable routines

- His emotional patterns showed greatest engagement when helping others understand difficult topics

Rather than making dramatic overnight changes, Alex began a gradual realignment process:

1. He started a side project creating financial education content for young adults, combining his expertise with his communication strengths

2. He restructured his work schedule to allow for one "exploration day" each month to pursue new interests

3. He had honest conversations with his partner about his emerging self-understanding

4. He adjusted his home environment to include more creative spaces

Over 18 months, these small changes led to greater alignment. Eventually, Alex transitioned to running his educational platform full-time, combining his financial expertise with his true strengths and values. His income initially decreased but his fulfilment and energy dramatically increased.

Most importantly, Alex shifted from living according to external expectations to making choices based on self-knowledge. This internal freedom created external options he hadn't previously imagined.

Conclusion

Self-discovery—understanding who you are and what you want—forms the foundation for breaking free from feeling stuck. Without this knowledge, you risk building someone else's dream rather than creating a life that truly fits you.

By developing self-awareness, practicing self-acceptance, and committing to self-alignment, you create the conditions for authentic success and genuine freedom. Your choices become expressions of your true nature rather than reactions to external pressures.

Remember: You don't need to have all the answers immediately. Self-discovery unfolds gradually as you pay attention to what energizes you, what matters most, and what feels like coming home to yourself. In the next chapter, we'll build on this foundation with a practical tool for assessing your current situation across all four life pillars: The 4 Life Pillars Audit.

1.4 The 4 Life Pillars Audit

Now that you've begun the journey of self-discovery, it's time to take an honest look at where you currently stand in each area of life. This assessment isn't about judgment or comparison—it's about clarity. You can't create a roadmap to your destination without first understanding your starting point.

The 4 Life Pillars Audit provides a comprehensive framework for evaluating your current situation in the four fundamental dimensions that support a fulfilling life: Health, Wealth, Relationships, and Purpose. This structured assessment will help you identify which areas need the most attention and provide a baseline for measuring your progress as you implement the strategies in this book.

Why a Comprehensive Life Audit Matters

Before diving into the assessment, let's understand why evaluating all four pillars simultaneously is so powerful:

1. Reveals Interdependencies: The four pillars don't exist in isolation. Health affects your energy for building wealth and relationships. Financial stress impacts health and the time available for meaningful relationships. Each area influences the others in complex ways.

2. Prevents Tunnel Vision: Without a balanced perspective, it's easy to hyperfocus on one area (often career or finances) while neglecting others. This tunnel vision eventually leads to problems that cannot be solved within that single domain.

3. Identifies Root Causes: Sometimes what appears to be a problem in one area actually stems from issues in another. For example, relationship difficulties might result from lack of purpose, or health problems might stem from financial stress.

4. Optimizes Resource Allocation: Your time, energy, and attention are limited resources. A comprehensive audit helps you invest these resources where they'll create the greatest positive impact in your life.

5. Creates a Balanced Vision: True success requires harmony across all four dimensions. The audit helps you develop an integrated vision rather than compartmentalized goals.

The 4 Life Pillars Explained

Before conducting your audit, let's clarify what each pillar encompasses:

1. Health Pillar

Health isn't merely the absence of illness but a state of complete physical, mental, and emotional well-being. This pillar includes:

- **Physical Health**: Energy levels, fitness, nutrition, sleep quality, and absence of illness

- **Mental Health**: Cognitive function, focus, learning capacity, and mental clarity

- **Emotional Health**: Emotional awareness, regulation, resilience, and overall psychological well-being

2. Wealth Pillar

Wealth represents your relationship with money and resources. This pillar encompasses:

- **Income Generation**: Your ability to create financial resources through work, business, investments, etc.

- **Financial Management**: How effectively you budget, save, and allocate resources

- **Financial Independence**: Your progress toward having enough resources to make choices based on values rather than necessity

- **Wealth Mindset**: Your beliefs and emotions around money and abundance

3. Relationships Pillar

This pillar concerns the quality of your connections with others, including:

- **Intimate Relationships**: Partnership, family, and closest friendships

- **Social Connections**: Broader friendship networks and community involvement

- **Professional Relationships**: Connections with colleagues, clients, mentors, etc.

- **Relationship with Self**: Your internal relationship characterized by self-awareness, acceptance, and compassion

4. Purpose Pillar

Purpose encompasses meaning, direction, and fulfillment in your activities. This pillar includes:

- **Career Fulfillment**: Alignment between your work and your values, strengths, and interests

- **Contribution**: How you make a difference to others and causes you care about

- **Personal Growth**: Continuous development of your capabilities and character

- **Life Meaning**: Your sense of why you're here and what makes your life worthwhile

Conducting Your Life Pillars Audit

Now, let's conduct a thorough assessment of each pillar in your life. For each category, you'll answer specific questions, rate your current satisfaction level, and identify strengths and growth areas.

Exercise: Comprehensive Life Pillars Audit

Health Pillar Assessment

Answer each question honestly, then rate your overall satisfaction with this area from 1-10 (where 1 =completely dissatisfied and 10 = completely satisfied).

Physical Health:

How is your energy level throughout the day?

How consistent are you with exercise and physical activity?

How would you describe your nutritional habits?

How would you rate your sleep quality and consistency?

Do you have any physical health concerns currently?

Physical Health Satisfaction Rating (1-10): _________

Mental Health:

How would you describe your ability to focus and concentrate?

How well do you manage stress in your daily life?

Do you regularly experience mental clarity and sharp thinking?

How would you describe your learning habits and intellectual growth?

Do you experience anxiety, depression, or other mental health challenges?

Mental Health Satisfaction Rating (1-10): _________

Emotional Health:

How aware are you of your emotions as they arise?

How effectively do you manage difficult emotions?

How often do you experience positive emotions like joy, gratitude, and peace?

How resilient are you when facing life's challenges?

Do you have practices for emotional self-care?

Emotional Health Satisfaction Rating (1-10): _________

Overall, Health Pillar Rating (average of the three categories): _________

Health Pillar Strengths (What's working well?):_________________________

Health Pillar Growth Areas (What needs improvement?):_____________

Wealth Pillar Assessment

Income Generation:

How satisfied are you with your current income level?

How stable and predictable is your income?

Do you have multiple streams of income or rely on a single source?

How aligned is your income-generating work with your strengths and interests?

What opportunities do you see for increasing your income?

Income Generation Satisfaction Rating (1-10): _________

Financial Management:

Do you follow a budget or spending plan?

How would you describe your saving habits?

How effectively do you manage debt?

Do you have adequate emergency funds?

How knowledgeable are you about personal finance?

Financial Management Satisfaction Rating (1-10): _________

Financial Independence:

How dependent are you on your primary income source?

Do you have investments working for you?

How prepared are you for retirement or long-term financial security?

Could you survive financially if unable to work for several months?

How free do you feel to make important life decisions without financial constraints?

Financial Independence Satisfaction Rating (1-10):________

Overall Wealth Pillar Rating (average of the three categories): ________

Wealth Pillar Strengths (What's working well?):__________________

Wealth Pillar Growth Areas (What needs improvement?):____________

Relationships Pillar Assessment

Intimate Relationships:

How satisfied are you with your closest relationships (partner, family, best friends)?

How emotionally supported do you feel by your inner circle?

How authentic can you be in your closest relationships?

How effectively do you communicate in these relationships?

How well do you balance giving and receiving in close relationships?

Intimate Relationships Satisfaction Rating (1-10): _________

Social Connections:

How satisfied are you with your broader social network?

Do you have community groups or friendships that share your interests?

How often do you engage in meaningful social interaction?

Do you feel a sense of belonging in your communities?

How diverse and enriching is your social circle?

Social Connections Satisfaction Rating (1-10): _________

Professional Relationships:

How would you describe your relationships with colleagues?

Do you have mentors or supportive professional connections?

How effective is your professional network for opportunities and growth?

How respected do you feel in your professional environment?

Do you have positive relationships with clients, customers, or those you serve?

Professional Relationships Satisfaction Rating (1-10):_________

Overall Relationships Pillar Rating (average of the three categories): _______

Relationships Pillar Strengths (What's working well?):_______________

Relationships Pillar Growth Areas (What needs improvement?): ____________________

Purpose Pillar Assessment

Career Fulfilment:

How meaningful do you find your current work?

How well does your work utilize your natural strengths and talents?

Does your work environment align with your values?

How energized do you feel about your work/career direction?

Does your work provide appropriate challenge and growth?

Career Fulfilment Satisfaction Rating (1-10): _________

Contribution:

How satisfied are you with the positive difference you make in others' lives?

Are you contributing to causes or communities you care about?

Do you feel your unique gifts are being used to benefit others?

How well are you using your resources (time, money, skills) to contribute?

Do others benefit from your knowledge and capabilities?

Contribution Satisfaction Rating (1-10): _________

Personal Growth:

How committed are you to ongoing learning and development?

Are you regularly challenging yourself to grow?

Do you have clear growth goals and development plans?

How well do you learn from experiences, including failures?

Are you becoming more of the person you want to be?

Personal Growth Satisfaction Rating (1-10): _________

Overall Purpose Pillar Rating (average of the three categories): _______

Purpose Pillar Strengths (What's working well?):_____________________

Purpose Pillar Growth Areas (What needs improvement?): _________

Interpreting Your Audit Results

After completing the comprehensive audit for all four pillars, it's time to analyse the results and identify patterns:

1. Create Your Life Pillar Profile

Transfer your overall ratings for each pillar to create your current profile:

Health Pillar Rating: ______

Wealth Pillar Rating: ______

Relationships Pillar Rating: ______

Purpose Pillar Rating: ______

2. Identify Your Strongest and Weakest Pillars

Your strongest pillar (highest rating): _____________________

Your weakest pillar (lowest rating): _____________________

3. Look for Imbalances and Connections

Are there significant gaps between your pillars? A difference of 3 or more points between pillars often indicates an imbalance that requires attention. Consider how your weaker pillars might be affecting the stronger ones, and vice versa.

4. Distinguish Between Satisfaction and Importance

For each pillar, consider not just your current satisfaction level but also how important this area is to you. Sometimes an area with a moderate rating requires immediate attention because it's highly important to your overall well-being and goals.

Journal Prompt: Priority Reflection

For each pillar, reflect on these questions:

1. How important is this pillar to my overall sense unfulfillment right now?

2. How would improvements in this area positively impact other areas of my life?

3. What would become possible if I significantly strengthened this pillar?

Planning Your Next Steps

Based on your audit results, you can now create a strategic approach for breaking free from feeling stuck:

1. The Weakest Pillar Approach

Often, the most effective strategy is to focus first on your weakest pillar, especially if it's significantly lower than the others. Strengthening this foundation can create positive ripple effects throughout your life.

For example, if Health is your weakest pillar, addressing energy, sleep, and stress management might improve your performance in work (Wealth), enhance your mood in relationships, and provide clarity about your purpose.

2. The Critical Few Approach

Rather than trying to improve everything at once, identify 2-3specific subcategories across your pillars that would create the most significant positive impact if improved. These "leverage points" often influence multiple areas simultaneously.

For example, you might focus on:

Sleep quality (Health) + Morning routine (Purpose) + Budget system (Wealth)

3. The Strength Amplification Approach

Sometimes the most efficient path forward is to leverage your strongest areas to improve weaker ones.

For example, if Relationships is your strongest pillar, you might:

Find a workout partner to improve your Health pillar

Join a mastermind group to enhance your Wealth strategies

Connect with inspiring mentors who help clarify your Purpose

Exercise: Strategic Action Plan

Based on your audit results, create an initial action plan:

1. Priority Pillar to focus on first: _______________________

2. Top 3 specific improvements to make in this pillar:

a. _____________________

b. _____________________

c. _____________________

3. One small action to take in the next 24 hours for each improvement:

Action for improvement a: _____________________

Action for improvement b: ________________________

Action for improvement c: ________________________

The Pillars in Action: Case Studies

Case Study 1: Sarah's Health-First Approach

Sarah's Life Pillar Profile:

Health: 4/10

Wealth: 7/10

Relationships: 6/10

Purpose: 5/10

Sarah was a marketing manager with a decent salary but constantly felt exhausted and overwhelmed. Her audit revealed that health was her weakest pillar—she was sleeping poorly, skipping meals, and experiencing chronic stress.

Instead of pushing harder in her career, Sarah focused on rebuilding her health foundation first. She:

Created a non-negotiable sleep schedule (10pm-6am)

Implemented a simple morning routine with 20 minutes of movement

Prepared healthy lunches for the workweek every Sunday

Took three 5-minute breathing breaks during her workday

Within six weeks, her energy had significantly improved. This created a positive cascade effect: With more energy, she performed better at work, had more patience in relationships, and gained clarity about her career direction. The health pillar became the foundation for improvements across all other areas.

Case Study 2: Michael's Purpose-Driven Transformation

Michael's Life Pillar Profile:

Health: 6/10

Wealth: 7/10

Relationships: 8/10Purpose: 3/10

Michael had a stable corporate job, good health habits, and strong relationships, but felt deeply unfulfilled. His audit revealed a significant deficiency in the Purpose pillar—particularly in career alignment and contribution.

Michael's approach focused on finding greater meaning while maintaining stability in his other pillars:

He volunteered his professional skills with a nonprofit once per week

He initiated a side project aligning with his values and interests

He had conversations with five people working in fields he found interesting

He began a daily practice of identifying the most meaningful moment each day

These purpose-oriented actions gradually clarified his direction. Over 10 months, Michael transitioned to a role with greater alignment—one that utilized his skills while contributing to causes he cared about. Though his salary initially decreased slightly, his overall fulfilment increased dramatically, and he found himself more motivated to manage his finances strategically.

Making the Audit a Regular Practice

The 4 Life Pillars Audit isn't meant to be a one-time exercise. To create sustainable change, consider:

Quarterly Check-ins: Set calendar reminders to revisit your audit every three months. This allows you to track progress, notice changes, and make adjustments to your approach.   **Annual Deep Dive**: Once a year, conduct a comprehensive audit and reflection. This broader perspective helps you recognize patterns and shifts that might not be visible in shorter timeframes.

Life Transition Audits: Whenever you experience a significant life change (job transition, relationship shift, health event, etc.), revisit the audit to recalibrate your understanding of your current state.

Conclusion

The 4 Life Pillars Audit provides a clear, comprehensive picture of your current situation across the dimensions that matter most for a fulfilled life. This clarity is essential forbreaking free from feeling stuck and creating meaningful change.

Remember that improvement doesn't happen all at once. By identifying your starting point, understanding the interconnections between different life areas, and focusing on strategic leverage points, you can begin creating positive momentum that builds over time.

In the next section of this book, we'll dive deeper into the first pillar: Health – Your Foundation for Success. You'll discover practical strategies for building physical energy, mental fitness, and emotional strength to support your journey toward freedom and fulfilment.

Conclusion

As we reach the end of our journey together, I hope this book has provided you with the insights, tools, and inspiration needed to break free from feeling stuck and create a life of genuine freedom and success.

Remember that transformation isn't an event—it's a process. There will be challenges, setbacks, and moments of doubt along the way. What matters is not perfection but persistence. Each small step you take toward greater alignment with your authentic self and balanced growth across the four life pillars brings you closer to the life you truly desire.

The strategies and principles in this book aren't theoretical concepts—they're practical approaches that have helped countless individuals transform their lives. I've witnessed people move from financial struggle to abundance, from illness to vibrant health, from toxic relationships to nurturing connections, and from confusion to purposeful direction.

As you continue your journey beyond these pages, keep these final thoughts in mind:

Trust Your Timing: Your path doesn't need to look like anyone else's. Some changes happen quickly, while others unfold gradually. Trust that you're exactly where you need to be on your unique journey.

Celebrate Progress: Take time to acknowledge and celebrate how far you've come, not just how far you have to go. Every positive change, no matter how small, deserves recognition.

Embrace Continuous Learning: Stay curious and open to new ideas, approaches, and perspectives. The most successful people are those who never stop learning and growing.

Maintain Balance: Regularly check in with all four life pillars to ensure you're creating holistic success rather than achieving in one area at the expense of others.

Share Your Journey: As you experience transformation, share your insights and encouragement with others. Your story might be exactly what someone else needs to hear to begin their own journey toward freedom.

Finally, remember that breaking free is both a destination Anda way of being. True freedom isn't just about external circumstances—it's an internal state of authenticity, courage, and alignment that you carry with you regardless of what's happening around you.

I believe in your capacity to create a life of genuine success and freedom. The fact that you've engaged with this book demonstrates your commitment to growth and your desire for something more. That commitment and desire, combined with the strategies you've learned, provide everything you need to transform your life.

The path ahead is yours to create. Make it beautiful, make it meaningful, and most importantly, make it authentically yours.

2. Health: Your Foundation Of Success

In the previous section, we explored the four pillars that form the foundation of a fulfilled life—Health, Wealth, Relationships, and Purpose. Now, we'll dive deep into the first and most important pillar: Health.

Why start with health? Because without a strong, energetic body and a clear, focused mind, achieving success in any other area becomes significantly harder. Have you ever tried to be productive while sick or tired? Have you noticed how stress affects your decision-making? Your health is the engine that powers everything else in your life.

The truth that many success gurus don't emphasize enough is this: **your physical and mental condition directly impacts your ability to create wealth, build relationships, and fulfill your purpose.** This is why the world's most successful people—from CEOs like Jeff Bezos to thought leaders like Robin Sharma—prioritize their health above almost everything else.

In this section, we'll explore four key aspects of health that directly impact your success:

1. **Building Physical Energy** - Creating a strong, energetic body that supports your goals

2. **Mental Fitness & Emotional Strength** - Developing resilience and emotional intelligence

3. **Daily Practices for a Healthy, Productive Mind** - Routines and habits that optimize your thinking

4. **Overcoming Stress, Anxiety & Overthinking** - Practical strategies to overcome common mental barriers

What makes this approach different from typical health advice is that we're not focusing on health for the sake of health alone. Instead, we're approaching health as a strategic asset—a foundation that enables you to perform at your best in every area of life.

2.1 Building Physical Energy

Energy, not time, is your most valuable resource. We all have the same 24 hours in a day, but our energy levels determine how much we can accomplish within those hours and how effectively we can perform.

Robin Sharma, who has coached some of the world's top CEOs and leaders, often says: *"Energy is even more important than intelligence."* This might sound surprising, but think about it—what good is being smart if you're constantly exhausted, unfocused, or burned out?

Understanding Your Energy Systems

Your physical energy comes from four interconnected sources, and each needs to be optimized for peak performance:

1. **Physical Movement** - How you use and strengthen your body

2. **Nutrition** - The fuel you provide your body

3. **Sleep** - Your body's recovery and restoration period

4. **Breath** - The most immediate energy source

1. Physical Movement: Beyond Exercise

Regular physical activity is non-negotiable for anyone seeking success. But this doesn't mean you need to become a fitness enthusiast or spend hours at the gym.

Physical movement provides benefits far beyond physical appearance. Studies show that regular exercise:

- Increases mental alertness and cognitive function

- Reduces symptoms of anxiety and depression

- Improves sleep quality

- Boosts creativity and problem-solving abilities

- Enhances mood through the release of endorphins

CASE STUDY: How Movement Transformed a CEO's Performance

John, a CEO of a mid-sized technology company, was working 70+ hours per week. Despite his intelligence and work ethic, he found himself constantly fatigued, irritable, and making poor decisions. His solution was always "more coffee and longer hours."

After suffering from burnout, John reluctantly followed the advice to prioritize daily movement. He started with just 20 minutes of walking each morning before checking his email. Within two weeks, he reported higher energy levels, better mood, and clearer thinking. Within three months, he had reduced his working hours while increasing productivity by delegating more effectively—a decision he attributes to his clearer mental state from regular movement.

Most importantly, his team noted a significant improvement in his leadership style, as his improved mood and energy made him more approachable and better at listening.

The Minimum Effective Dose for Movement

You don't need to become an athlete to get the energy-boosting benefits of movement. Research shows that even modest amounts of physical activity can significantly impact your energy and cognitive function.

Here's what I recommend as a starting point:

- **Daily Movement**: 20-30 minutes of any physical activity that raises your heart rate (walking, cycling, dancing, etc.)

- **Strength Training**: 2-3 sessions per week (even bodyweight exercises like push-ups, squats, and planks are effective)

- **Movement Breaks**: 5-minute breaks every 60-90 minutes during work (stretch, walk, or do quick exercises)

EXERCISE: Your Personal Movement Audit

Take a moment to assess your current movement patterns:

1. How many minutes of intentional physical activity do you get each day?

2. How many hours do you spend sitting without moving?

3. Do you feel energized or depleted after your typical day?

4. What type of movement do you actually enjoy?

Now, identify ONE small change you can make today to increase your physical movement. Remember, the best exercise is the one you'll actually do consistently.

2. Nutrition: Food as Fuel and Medicine

What you eat directly impacts your energy, focus, mood, and long-term health. The right nutritional approach can dramatically increase your productivity and mental clarity.

Jim Rohn said it best: *"Take care of your body. It's the only place you have to live."* While there are countless diet philosophies, here are the fundamental principles that apply to everyone seeking optimal energy:

The Energy Nutrition Principles

- **Eat Real Food**: Minimize processed foods and maximize whole, unprocessed foods

- **Balance Blood Sugar**: Avoid energy crashes by combining protein, healthy fats, and complex carbohydrates

- **Stay Hydrated**: Even mild dehydration can decrease cognitive function by up to 20%

- **Mind Your Gut**: Gut health directly impacts brain function through the gut-brain axis

- **Timing Matters**: When you eat can be as important as what you eat

The High-Performance Eating Pattern

Rather than recommending a specific diet, I suggest focusing on an eating pattern that supports sustained energy:

1. **Start With Protein**: Begin each day with a protein-rich breakfast to stabilize blood sugar and provide lasting energy

2. **Hydrate Before Caffeine**: Drink 16-20oz of water before your morning coffee or tea

3. **Power-Packed Meals**: Include protein, healthy fats, fiber, and colorful vegetables at each meal

4. **Strategic Snacking**: If energy dips between meals, choose snacks combining protein and healthy fats (like nuts with fruit or Greek yogurt)

5. **Mind The Evening**: Eat lighter at night and finish eating 2-3 hours before bedtime for better sleep

ACTION STEP: The 3-Day Energy Reset

For the next three days, try this simple nutrition reset to experience how food affects your energy:

- Start each day with 20oz of water

- Include protein at every meal and snack

- Eat a vegetable or fruit at every meal

- Eliminate added sugar and processed foods

- Stop eating 3 hours before bedtime

Track your energy levels throughout the day on a scale of 1-10. Many people report significantly higher and more stable energy by day three.

3. Sleep: Your Ultimate Recovery Tool

In our hustle culture, sleep is often the first thing sacrificed in the pursuit of success. This approach is not just counterproductive—it's dangerous to your health and detrimental to your success.

Arianna Huffington, who collapsed from exhaustion while building her media empire, now calls sleep "a performance enhancement tool." After her wake-up call, she transformed her approach to sleep and wrote an entire book on its importance for success.

Here's what the research shows about sleep and performance:

- Sleep deprivation impairs judgment, decision-making, and creativity

- Just one night of poor sleep can reduce cognitive function by 20-30%

- Chronic sleep deprivation increases the risk of serious health conditions

- Sleep is when your brain consolidates learning and memories

- Quality sleep improves emotional regulation and stress management

Sleep Quality Over Quantity

While most adults need 7-9 hours of sleep, quality is just as important as quantity. Here are strategies to improve your sleep quality:

The Sleep Optimization Protocol

1. **Consistent Schedule**: Go to bed and wake up at the same time daily

2. **Light Management**: Get morning sunlight exposure and limit blue light from screens in the evening

3. **Environment Optimization**: Keep your bedroom cool (65-68°F/18-20°C), dark, and quiet

4. **Wind-Down Ritual**: Create a 30-minute pre-sleep routine to signal your body it's time to rest

5. **Nutrition Timing**: Avoid large meals, alcohol, and caffeine close to bedtime

"Sleep is the greatest legal performance-enhancing drug that most people are neglecting."
— Matthew Walker, Ph.D., Sleep Scientist and Author of "Why We Sleep"

CASE STUDY: The CEO Who Added $3 Million in Revenue by Sleeping More

Sarah, the founder of a marketing agency, prided herself on working 16-hour days and only sleeping 4-5 hours per night. Her company was successful but had plateaued, and she was experiencing frequent migraines and mood swings.

After reading about the cognitive impacts of sleep deprivation, she decided to experiment with prioritizing sleep for 90 days. She committed to 8 hours in bed each night, created a wind-down ritual, and stopped working after 9 PM.

The results surprised even her. Not only did her energy and mood improve dramatically, but her decision-making abilities sharpened. She identified inefficiencies in her business that she had previously missed, restructured her team, and focused on higher-value clients. Within six months, her company added $3 million in new revenue—all while she worked fewer hours than before.

Her conclusion: "I wasn't working smart because I was too tired to see the obvious solutions."

4. Breath: Your Instant Energy Switch

Your breath is the most immediate tool you have for influencing your energy and mental state. Most people breathe in shallow, rapid patterns, especially when stressed or focused on work. This breathing pattern activates your sympathetic nervous system (the "fight-or-flight" response), which can leave you feeling anxious and depleted.

Strategic breathing practices can:

- Instantly increase energy and alertness when needed

- Calm your nervous system during stressful situations

- Improve oxygen delivery to your brain and muscles

- Enhance focus and concentration

- Reduce anxiety and racing thoughts

The Two Essential Breathing Techniques

These two simple techniques should be in everyone's energy management toolkit:

EXERCISE: Box Breathing for Calm Energy

Used by Navy SEALs, executives, and performers to stay calm under pressure:

1. Inhale through your nose for a count of 4

2. Hold your breath for a count of 4

3. Exhale through your mouth for a count of 4

4. Hold with empty lungs for a count of 4

5. Repeat 3-5 times

When to use it: Before important meetings, when feeling stressed, or when transitioning between tasks.

EXERCISE: Energizing Breath

For a quick boost of energy and alertness without caffeine:

1. Sit up straight with shoulders relaxed

2. Inhale deeply through your nose

3. Exhale forcefully through your mouth in short, powerful bursts (like you're blowing out candles), pulling in your abdomen with each exhale

4. Repeat for 10-15 exhales

5. Finish with 3 deep breaths

When to use it: During the afternoon energy slump, before a workout, or when you need to focus on an important task.

Creating Your Energy Management System

Now that we've covered the four physical energy sources, it's time to create your personal energy management system. Remember, small changes implemented consistently will outperform dramatic overhauls that don't last.

The 3 Levels of Energy Management

I recommend implementing energy management practices at three levels:

Level	Timeframe	Practices
Daily	Every day	- Morning movement routine (10-30 minutes) - Strategic meal timing and composition

		- Breathing techniques between tasks - Consistent sleep schedule
Weekly	Once per week	- 1-2 more intense strength training sessions - Meal preparation for the upcoming week - One full day of recovery (minimal work, more rest) - Weekly energy audit (what drained/boosted your energy?)
Quarterly	Every 3 months	- 3-7 day nutritional reset - Fitness reassessment and goal setting - Sleep quality optimization - Learning new energy management techniques

ACTION STEP: Your Minimum Effective Dose

Based on the information in this chapter, identify the smallest steps you can take in each area that would make the biggest difference in your energy:

1. **Movement**: What is one movement practice you can commit to daily? (Example: 20-minute morning walk)

2. **Nutrition**: What is one eating habit you can change this week? (Example: Protein-rich breakfast)

3. **Sleep**: What is one change to improve your sleep quality? (Example: No screens 1 hour before bed)

4. **Breath**: When will you practice one of the breathing techniques daily? (Example: Box breathing before meetings)

Write these down and commit to implementing them for the next 21 days.

"Take care of your body. It's the only place you have to live in."
— Jim Rohn

Key Takeaways: Building Physical Energy

1. Physical energy is the foundation that enables all other forms of success

2. Movement, nutrition, sleep, and breath are your four primary energy sources

3. Small, consistent improvements across all four areas will transform your energy

4. Energy management requires daily attention but not necessarily large time investments

5. High energy is a competitive advantage in today's demanding world

Remember, the goal isn't perfection. The goal is to create sustainable energy management practices that support your success journey. Start small, be consistent, and adjust as needed based on your results.

In the next chapter, we'll build on this physical foundation by exploring mental fitness and emotional strength—the psychological assets that allow you to perform at your best even under pressure.

2.2 Mental Fitness & Emotional Strength

While physical energy forms the foundation of success, your mental and emotional capabilities determine how effectively you use that energy. Think of physical energy as the fuel in your tank, while mental fitness and emotional strength represent your ability to navigate the road ahead—especially when that road gets bumpy.

In this chapter, we'll explore how to develop these critical internal resources that separate those who thrive under pressure from those who crumble when challenges arise.

What Is Mental Fitness?

Mental fitness refers to your mind's ability to perform optimally—to focus, think clearly, make decisions, and stay resilient when faced with challenges. Just like physical fitness, mental fitness must be built through consistent training and practice.

The components of mental fitness include:

- **Focus**: The ability to direct and maintain attention where it's most valuable

- **Cognitive Flexibility**: The capacity to adapt your thinking in response to new information

- **Mental Stamina**: The endurance to sustain mental effort over time

- **Decision Quality**: The skill of making good choices, especially under pressure

- **Learning Agility**: The speed at which you acquire and apply new knowledge

What Is Emotional Strength?

Emotional strength is your ability to understand, manage, and leverage your emotions—rather than being controlled by them. It includes:

- **Emotional Awareness**: Recognizing your emotions as they arise

- **Emotional Regulation**: Managing strong emotions effectively

- **Emotional Resilience**: Bouncing back from setbacks and disappointments

- **Emotional Intelligence**: Understanding and influencing the emotions of others

- **Emotional Courage**: Facing difficult emotions rather than avoiding them

Together, mental fitness and emotional strength create what psychologists call "psychological capital"—an internal resource that helps you navigate challenges, recover from setbacks, and perform consistently at your best.

"Between stimulus and response, there is a space. In that space lies our freedom and power to choose our response. In our response lies our growth and our freedom."
— Viktor Frankl

The Science of Mental Fitness

Recent advances in neuroscience have revealed that our brains are far more adaptable than previously thought. Through a process called neuroplasticity, our brain physically changes in response to how we use it. This means mental fitness can be trained just like physical fitness.

Here's what research tells us about developing mental fitness:

- The brain strengthens neural pathways that are used frequently (the "neurons that fire together, wire together" principle)

- Challenging mental activities create new connections between neurons

- Rest and recovery are essential for mental performance, just as they are for physical performance

- Attention can be trained through practice, just like a muscle

- The brain's executive function (which handles complex planning, decision-making, and focus) can be strengthened through specific exercises

Building Your Mental Fitness Practice

Let's explore five key practices that will strengthen your mental fitness:

1. Focused Attention Training

In our distraction-filled world, the ability to focus deeply is becoming increasingly rare—and therefore increasingly valuable. Deep focus allows you to solve complex problems, learn more effectively, and produce higher quality work.

EXERCISE: The Focus Ladder

This exercise progressively builds your focus capacity:

1. Select a single task requiring concentration (reading, writing, problem-solving)

2. Start with just 5 minutes of complete focus (no phone, no distractions)

3. Use a timer and don't stop until it rings

4. Every few days, increase your focus time by 5 minutes

5. Work up to 50-90 minute focused sessions

When your mind wanders (and it will), gently bring your attention back to the task. Each time you do this, you're strengthening your "focus muscle."

2. Decision Quality Training

Every day, you make countless decisions that shape your life and success. Improving your decision-making process even slightly can have enormous benefits over time.

ACTION STEP: The Decision Journal

For important decisions, use this simple framework:

1. **The Decision**: What exactly are you deciding?

2. **The Context**: What's the situation requiring this decision?

3. **The Options**: What choices do you have?

4. **The Pros/Cons**: List the benefits and drawbacks of each option

5. **Your Mental State**: Are you tired, emotional, or clear-headed?

6. **The Decision**: What did you decide and why?

After implementation, revisit your journal to see what you can learn:

- Was the outcome what you expected?

- What would you do differently next time?

- Were there any cognitive biases influencing your decision?

This practice builds the metacognitive skills that improve future decisions.

3. Cognitive Flexibility Training

Cognitive flexibility—the ability to adapt your thinking based on new information—is essential in our rapidly changing world. People with high cognitive flexibility solve problems more creatively and adapt more effectively to change.

EXERCISE: The Alternative Perspectives Practice

For any challenge or problem you're facing:

1. Write down your current perspective and assumptions

2. Now, write at least three completely different perspectives on the same situation

3. For each alternative perspective, list what evidence might support it

4. Ask: "What would I do differently if this alternative view were true?"

This exercise trains your brain to see situations from multiple angles, expanding your thinking beyond habitual patterns.

4. Mental Recovery Practices

Just as physical muscles need recovery time, your brain requires downtime to consolidate learning and restore mental energy. Many high performers neglect this crucial aspect, leading to cognitive fatigue and diminished performance.

Effective mental recovery practices include:

- **Mindfulness Meditation**: Even 10 minutes daily can reduce mental fatigue and increase cognitive function

- **Nature Exposure**: "Attention Restoration Theory" shows that time in nature replenishes cognitive resources

- **Task Alternation**: Switching between different types of mental activities (analytical, creative, administrative) reduces cognitive strain

- **Strategic Breaks**: A 5-minute break every 25-50 minutes of intense mental work improves overall productivity

5. Learning Optimization

In today's knowledge economy, your ability to learn quickly and effectively is perhaps your most valuable skill. The good news is that learning itself is a learnable skill.

ACTION STEP: The Learning Accelerator Method

Apply these evidence-based learning principles to anything you want to master:

1. **Spaced Repetition**: Instead of cramming information, space out your learning over time (review materials after 1 day, 3 days, 1 week, etc.)

2. **Active Recall**: Test yourself on the material rather than simply reviewing it (close the book and try to explain concepts in your own words)

3. **Chunking**: Break complex information into manageable chunks, mastering each before moving on

4. **Teaching**: Explain what you're learning to someone else (or even to an imaginary student)

5. **Application**: Immediately apply new knowledge in a practical way

Choose one new skill or knowledge area and apply these principles for the next 30 days. You'll be amazed at how much more effectively you learn.

The Science of Emotional Strength

Our emotions are not random occurrences but sophisticated information-processing systems that help us navigate our world. Research in affective neuroscience shows that emotions:

- Provide valuable data about our environment and relationships

- Influence decision-making, often in beneficial ways

- Motivate action and help establish priorities

- Facilitate social connection and communication

- Can be regulated through various strategies

The goal isn't to eliminate emotions—even difficult ones—but to develop a healthy relationship with them. Emotional strength means using emotions as information while not being controlled by them.

Building Your Emotional Strength Practice

Let's explore five essential practices for developing emotional strength:

1. Emotional Awareness Training

You can't manage what you don't recognize. Many people operate on emotional autopilot, reacting to feelings without clearly identifying them. Increasing your emotional vocabulary and awareness is the first step toward emotional strength.

EXERCISE: The Emotion Tracking Practice

For one week, set a timer to go off randomly 3-5 times per day. When it does:

1. Pause and notice what emotion(s) you're experiencing

2. Name the emotion specifically (beyond just "good" or "bad")

3. Note the intensity (1-10) and any physical sensations

4. Identify what might have triggered this emotion

5. Observe without judgment or trying to change anything

This practice develops your "emotional radar," making you more aware of your emotional landscape throughout the day.

2. Emotional Regulation Strategies

Emotional regulation is not about suppressing emotions but about responding to them skillfully. Different situations call for different regulation strategies.

Key emotional regulation approaches include:

- **Cognitive Reappraisal**: Changing how you think about a situation to change how you feel about it

- **Acceptance**: Allowing emotions to be present without fighting them

- **Problem-Solving**: Taking action to address the source of the emotion

- **Attention Deployment**: Directing focus away from or toward emotional stimuli

- **Response Modulation**: Changing your behavioral response to an emotion

ACTION STEP: The Emotion Regulation Toolkit

Create your personal toolkit of strategies for difficult emotions:

For Anxiety/Fear:

- Box breathing (4 counts in, hold 4, out 4, hold 4)

- Realistic assessment of threats ("What's the actual likelihood?")

- Progressive muscle relaxation

For Anger/Frustration:

- Temporary physical distance ("I'll address this after a 10-minute walk")

- Perspective-taking ("What might they be experiencing?")

- Energy release (physical movement)

For Sadness/Disappointment:

- Self-compassion practice

- Social connection (reaching out to supportive people)

- Meaning-making ("What can I learn from this?")

The next time you experience a strong emotion, experiment with different regulation strategies to find what works best for you in different contexts.

3. Emotional Resilience Building

Resilience is your ability to bounce back from difficulties and adapt to changing circumstances. It's not a fixed trait but a set of skills that can be developed.

CASE STUDY: Building Resilience Through Adversity

Maya, a software engineer, was devastated when her startup failed after three years of intensive work. She had invested her savings, time, and identity in the venture, and its failure triggered depression and self-doubt.

Rather than rushing into another project, Maya took time to process her experience. She worked with a coach who helped her identify the specific skills she had developed and the valuable lessons from the failure. She practiced gratitude daily, focusing on what remained intact in her life despite the business loss.

Most importantly, she reframed the experience from "I am a failure" to "This specific venture didn't succeed, and that's given me invaluable experience." Within six months, she had secured a leadership position at a growing company, bringing her entrepreneurial mindset to her new role. Two years later, she launched a new startup that became profitable within its first year.

Maya credits her resilience practices with not just helping her recover but actually transforming the failure into a critical step in her ultimate success.

Key resilience-building practices include:

- **Post-Challenge Review**: Analyzing difficulties for learning and growth

- **Gratitude Practice**: Regularly acknowledging what's working and what you have

- **Realistic Optimism**: Balancing honest assessment with confidence in your ability to overcome

- **Meaning-Making**: Finding purpose and value in challenges

- **Support Utilization**: Effectively drawing on relationships during difficult times

4. Emotional Intelligence Development

Emotional intelligence—understanding and influencing emotions in yourself and others—is strongly correlated with success in leadership, relationships, and overall life satisfaction.

EXERCISE: The Empathy Builder

In your daily interactions for the next week:

1. Choose one conversation each day for focused empathy practice

2. During the conversation, make understanding the other person's emotions and perspective your primary goal

3. Ask questions that explore their feelings and viewpoint

4. Practice reflective listening by paraphrasing what you hear

5. Notice their non-verbal cues (facial expressions, body language, tone)

6. Temporarily set aside your own opinions and judgments

After each conversation, reflect: What emotions did you detect? What needs or values seemed important to them? How might their perspective differ from yours?

5. Emotional Courage Practice

Emotional courage is the willingness to experience difficult emotions when doing so serves your values and goals. Many people limit their potential by avoiding situations that might trigger uncomfortable feelings like fear, vulnerability, or uncertainty.

ACTION STEP: The Courage Expansion Exercise

This practice gradually expands your capacity for emotional discomfort:

1. Identify one area where emotional discomfort is limiting you (e.g., fear of rejection, discomfort with conflict, anxiety about public speaking)

2. Create a "courage ladder" with 5-7 steps of increasing challenge

3. Start with the lowest rung—something mildly uncomfortable but doable

4. Before each step, acknowledge the emotions that may arise and commit to experiencing them

5. After each step, reflect on what you learned and how you handled the emotions

6. Move to the next level only when you've integrated the learning from the previous step

For example, if you fear public speaking, your ladder might start with speaking up in a small meeting and gradually progress to giving a presentation to a larger group.

Key Takeaways: Mental Fitness & Emotional Strength

1. Mental fitness and emotional strength are trainable skills, not fixed traits

2. Regular, intentional practice in these areas creates lasting neural changes

3. Different situations require different mental and emotional strategies

4. Self-awareness is the foundation for both mental and emotional development

5. The goal is not to eliminate difficulties but to develop the capacity to navigate them effectively

In the next chapter, we'll explore specific daily practices that integrate physical, mental, and emotional well-being to create a healthy, productive mind.

2.3 Daily Practices for a Healthy, Productive Mind

Now that we've explored the foundations of physical energy, mental fitness, and emotional strength, let's integrate these concepts into practical daily routines. In this chapter, we'll focus on specific practices you can implement immediately to optimize your mind for peak performance.

The most successful people in the world don't just work hard—they work smart by strategically managing their mental resources. Robin Sharma calls this "The 5 AM Club" principle: winning the morning to win the day. While you don't necessarily need to wake up at 5 AM, the principle of having intentional daily practices is critical for sustained success.

The Science of Daily Mental Performance

Research in cognitive science, neurobiology, and performance psychology reveals several key principles about optimal mental functioning:

- The brain follows predictable cycles of high and low energy (approximately 90-120 minute cycles known as ultradian rhythms)

- Willpower and decision-making ability are finite resources that deplete throughout the day (known as decision fatigue)

- The brain's pre-frontal cortex (responsible for executive functions) requires specific conditions to perform optimally

- Mental performance is significantly influenced by physiological factors like blood glucose levels, hydration, and oxygen consumption

- Attention is a trainable skill that improves with deliberate practice

Based on these scientific insights, let's explore seven daily practices that will transform your mental performance.

1. The Morning Mental Optimization Routine

How you start your day sets the tone for everything that follows. A strategic morning routine primes your brain for clarity, focus, and productive action.

EXERCISE: The 20-Minute Mind Morning

This simple morning sequence takes just 20 minutes but dramatically improves mental performance:

Minutes 1-5: Movement

- Quick physical activity to increase blood flow to the brain

- Options: jumping jacks, sun salutations, brisk walking, or gentle stretching

- Focus on getting oxygen flowing to wake up your brain

Minutes 6-10: Mindfulness

- Brief meditation or focused breathing

- Simply observe your breath and present moment experience

- This activates the parasympathetic nervous system and improves attentional control

Minutes 11-15: Meaning

- Review your core values, goals, and intentions for the day

- Write down three priorities that will make the day successful

- Visualize yourself accomplishing these priorities effectively

Minutes 16-20: Mastery

- Spend five minutes learning something new related to your goals

- Read a few pages of a book, listen to an educational podcast, or review notes

- This primes your brain for growth and signals that learning is a priority

Implement this routine before checking email, social media, or news to protect your mental space during the most valuable hours of the day.

2. Strategic Energy Management Throughout the Day

Rather than working in a continuous marathon, high performers work in focused sprints aligned with their natural energy cycles.

ACTION STEP: The Ultradian Performance System

Implement this rhythm for optimal mental performance:

1. **Track Your Energy**: For one week, rate your energy and focus (1-10) every hour to identify your natural peaks and dips

2. **Schedule By Energy**: Place your most demanding cognitive tasks during your peak energy periods

3. **Work in Focused Blocks**: Use the "90/20 Rule"—90 minutes of focused work followed by 20 minutes of genuine recovery

4. **Digital Boundaries**: During focus blocks, eliminate all distractions (notifications, email, messages)

5. **True Recovery**: During breaks, step away from screens and do something physically and mentally refreshing (walk, stretch, hydrate, brief meditation)

This approach works with your biology rather than against it, allowing you to maintain high performance throughout the day without burnout.

CASE STUDY: From Burnout to Sustainable Performance

Michael, a management consultant, was known for his ability to work long hours, often pulling 12-14 hour days with few breaks. While initially praised for his work ethic, he began experiencing symptoms of burnout—reduced quality of work, irritability, and eventually, memory problems.

After reading about ultradian rhythms, he experimented with a completely different approach. Instead of working continuously, he began structuring his day around 90-minute focused sessions with 20-30 minute breaks. During each focus block, he eliminated all distractions and worked on only one significant task.

The results surprised everyone, including Michael. Not only did he complete his work in fewer hours, but the quality of his thinking improved dramatically. His clients noticed his more innovative solutions, and his colleagues commented on his improved mood and energy. Most importantly, he regained his enthusiasm for his work and eliminated the signs of burnout.

Michael's key insight: "I used to think breaks were a luxury I couldn't afford. Now I understand they're a necessity I can't work without."

3. Mindfulness Integration

Mindfulness—the practice of present-moment awareness without judgment—has moved from spiritual monasteries to mainstream corporations for good reason. Research shows that regular mindfulness practice physically changes the brain in ways that enhance focus, reduce stress, and improve decision-making.

Companies like Google, Apple, and Goldman Sachs have implemented mindfulness programs after seeing the cognitive benefits.

EXERCISE: Micro-Mindfulness Practices

You don't need to meditate for hours to benefit from mindfulness. These micro-practices can be integrated throughout your day:

The 3-Breath Reset (30 seconds)

- Between tasks or meetings, take three conscious breaths

- On the first breath, notice your body sensations

- On the second breath, relax any tension

- On the third breath, set an intention for the next activity

The STOP Practice (1 minute)

- **S**top what you're doing

- **T**ake a breath

- **O**bserve your thoughts, feelings, and body sensations

- **P**roceed with awareness

Mindful Transitions (varies)

- Use everyday transitions (entering/leaving rooms, before meetings, before eating) as mindfulness triggers

- Take a moment to become fully present during these natural breaks

- Notice details of your environment you normally overlook

These practices take seconds but interrupt the autopilot mode many of us operate in, bringing more awareness and intentionality to our day.

4. Strategic Information Consumption

In the age of information overload, what you choose NOT to consume is as important as what you do consume. The average person is bombarded with the equivalent of 174 newspapers worth of information daily, and this constant input dramatically affects cognitive function.

ACTION STEP: The Mental Diet Protocol

Just as you'd be careful about what food you put in your body, be intentional about the information you feed your mind:

1. **Information Fasting**: Designate specific periods (e.g., first hour of the day, one day per week) as "input-free" times where you create rather than consume

2. **Content Curation**: Audit your information sources and eliminate those that leave you feeling drained, anxious, or unfocused

3. **Deep Over Shallow**: Replace some social media and news browsing with books, long-form articles, or documentaries that provide depth

4. **Active Consumption**: When consuming content, do so actively—take notes, reflect on what you're learning, consider how to apply it

5. **Digital Boundaries**: Create tech-free zones (bedroom, dinner table) and times (evenings, weekends) to allow mental processing time

Remember: Your attention is your most valuable asset. Treat it accordingly.

5. Cognitive Enhancement Practices

Beyond managing energy and information, you can actively train specific cognitive skills to enhance your mental performance.

EXERCISE: The Daily Cognitive Workout

Spend 10 minutes daily on one of these evidence-based cognitive enhancement exercises, rotating through them throughout the week:

Monday: Working Memory Training

- Dual N-Back exercises (available as free apps)

- Memorize a short list and recall it backward

- Remember a sequence of actions and repeat them

Tuesday: Creative Thinking

- Generate 10 alternative uses for a common object

- Connect three unrelated ideas or objects in a meaningful way

- Solve a problem from a completely different perspective

Wednesday: Processing Speed

- Speed reading practice (use a timer and track words per minute)

- Quick math calculations without calculators

- Word or number puzzles with a timer

Thursday: Cognitive Flexibility

- Task-switching exercises (alternate between two different tasks)

- Learn something outside your field of expertise

- Argue against your own viewpoint on a topic

Friday: Focused Attention

- Single-point meditation (focus on one object, sensation, or thought)

- Mindful observation of a complex object, noticing details

- Completion of a detailed task without interruption

This systematic rotation ensures you're developing all aspects of cognitive function rather than only those you naturally prefer.

6. Social Cognitive Practices

Our brains are fundamentally social organs, and our mental performance is significantly influenced by our social interactions. Strategic management of your social environment enhances cognitive function.

ACTION STEP: The Cognitive Environment Optimization

Implement these social practices to enhance your mental performance:

1. **Mastermind Participation**: Join or create a group that meets regularly to discuss ideas, solve problems, and share knowledge

2. **Teaching Practice**: Regularly explain concepts to others (teaching something requires deeper processing than merely learning it)

3. **Cognitive Diversity Exposure**: Intentionally engage with people who think differently from you

4. **Intellectual Sparring**: Engage in respectful debate to sharpen your thinking

5. **Accountability Partnerships**: Pair with someone to maintain commitment to mental practices

These social practices leverage the power of collective intelligence and social accountability to enhance your individual cognitive performance.

7. Evening Mental Reset Routine

Just as your morning routine sets you up for success, your evening routine prepares your brain for restorative rest and subconscious problem-solving during sleep.

EXERCISE: The 3R Evening Protocol

This 15-minute evening practice optimizes cognitive recovery and preparation:

Review (5 minutes)

- Reflect on the day's achievements, challenges, and lessons

- Note what went well and what could be improved

- This practice creates closure and prevents work thoughts from disrupting sleep

Release (5 minutes)

- Write down any lingering thoughts, concerns, or ideas

- Create tomorrow's priority list so your brain doesn't have to hold these items

- Practice forgiveness for any mistakes or regrets from the day

Recharge (5 minutes)

- Engage in a calming activity (reading, gentle stretching, gratitude practice)

- Avoid screens, which interfere with melatonin production

- Set a specific intention for your rest period

This routine signals to your brain that the workday is complete and it's safe to transition into restoration mode.

"You will never change your life until you change something you do daily. The secret of your success is found in your daily routine."
— John C. Maxwell

Integrating These Practices: The Minimum Effective Dose

While all seven practices would ideally be part of your routine, even implementing a few will significantly improve your mental performance. Here's a suggested approach for getting started:

Time Available	Priority Practices
If you have 15 minutes daily	Morning Mental Optimization Routine (simplified to 15 minutes)
If you have 30 minutes daily	Morning Mental Optimization (20 minutes) Micro-Mindfulness Practices throughout the day (5 minutes total) 3R Evening Protocol (simplified to 5 minutes)
If you have 60 minutes daily	Morning Mental Optimization (20 minutes) Strategic Energy Management with 90/20 work cycles Cognitive Enhancement Practice (10 minutes) 3R Evening Protocol (15 minutes)

ACTION STEP: Your Personalized Daily Mental Performance Plan

Based on the practices in this chapter, create your personalized plan:

1. Review all seven practices and rate them on a scale of 1-10 based on which would most benefit you right now

2. Select the top 2-3 practices to implement first

3. Schedule specific times for these practices in your calendar

4. Identify potential obstacles and create strategies to overcome them

5. Commit to a 21-day implementation period before evaluating and adjusting

Remember: Consistency with a few practices is more valuable than inconsistent attempts at many.

Key Takeaways: Daily Practices for a Healthy, Productive Mind

1. Your daily mental practices determine your long-term cognitive performance and success

2. Working with your brain's natural rhythms and biology increases productivity while reducing burnout

3. Short, consistent practices integrated throughout your day are more effective than occasional intensive efforts

4. What you choose not to do (information fasting, eliminating distractions) is as important as what you do

5. Intentional daily routines eliminate decision fatigue and create mental space for creative and strategic thinking

In the next chapter, we'll address one of the most common mental challenges in today's world: overcoming stress, anxiety, and overthinking. You'll learn practical strategies to transform these mental barriers into assets for growth and performance.

2.4 Overcoming Stress, Anxiety & Overthinking

In our fast-paced, high-pressure world, stress, anxiety, and overthinking have become common experiences. While these mental states are often portrayed as purely negative, the truth is more nuanced. The right amount of stress can enhance performance, anxiety often signals something important, and deep thinking is essential for solving complex problems.

The issue isn't the presence of these experiences but rather how we relate to them and manage them. In this chapter, we'll explore evidence-based strategies to transform these potential barriers into allies on your journey to success.

Understanding the Stress Response

Stress is your body's natural reaction to any demand or challenge. It triggers a cascade of hormones that prepare you to respond effectively. This system evolved to help us survive physical threats, but in modern life, it's activated by psychological challenges—deadlines, financial pressures, relationship conflicts, and uncertainty.

There are three important distinctions to understand about stress:

- **Acute vs. Chronic Stress**: Short-term stress can enhance performance, while prolonged stress damages health and cognitive function

- **Distress vs. Eustress**: Negative stress (distress) feels overwhelming and harmful, while positive stress (eustress) feels challenging but growth-promoting

- **Stress Response vs. Stress Recovery**: The activation of your stress response isn't inherently problematic—inadequate recovery is the real issue

"It's not stress that kills us, it is our reaction to it."
— Hans Selye, Pioneer of Stress Research

The Science of Anxiety and Overthinking

Anxiety and overthinking are related but distinct phenomena:

- **Anxiety** is an emotional state characterized by worry, tension, and often physical symptoms like racing heart or shallow breathing

- **Overthinking** is a cognitive pattern involving repetitive, often unproductive thought cycles (rumination about the past or worry about the future)

Both serve evolutionary purposes—anxiety alerts us to potential threats, while analytical thinking helps solve problems. But in modern life, these mechanisms often become overactivated, reducing rather than enhancing our effectiveness.

The good news? Neuroscience shows that we can rewire these responses through specific practices. Our brains remain plastic throughout life, allowing us to create new neural pathways that support more helpful responses to challenge and uncertainty.

Stress Mastery Strategies

Let's explore five evidence-based approaches to transform your relationship with stress:

1. Stress Reappraisal

Research from Harvard and Stanford shows that how you think about stress dramatically influences its impact. People who view stress as helpful (rather than harmful) show different physiological responses— their blood vessels remain relaxed, and they release more DHEA, a hormone that helps brain growth.

EXERCISE: The Stress Benefit Finding Practice

When facing a stressful situation:

1. Acknowledge the stress response in your body (increased heart rate, faster breathing, etc.)

2. Mentally reframe these sensations: "My body is energizing me to meet this challenge"

3. Identify the potential benefits of the stressor:

    o   What might this situation be preparing me for?

    o   What skills or strengths might I develop through this?

    o   How might overcoming this benefit me in the future?

4. Focus on the aspect of the situation you can control or influence

This isn't positive thinking or denial—it's a realistic assessment that acknowledges both challenges and opportunities.

2. Stress Recovery Programming

Elite athletes understand that training stress must be balanced with strategic recovery. The same principle applies to all forms of stress. Your ability to recover effectively determines whether stress depletes or strengthens you.

ACTION STEP: The Strategic Recovery System

Implement this three-tiered recovery system:

Micro-Recovery (1-5 minutes, several times daily)

- Deep breathing exercises between tasks

- Brief movement breaks (stretch, walk, simple exercises)

- Momentary sensory shifts (look out a window, listen to a favorite song)

Mid-Recovery (30-90 minutes, daily)

- Nature exposure (even brief time outdoors resets stress hormones)

- Physical activity that you enjoy

- Social connection with supportive people

- Mindfulness practice or meditation

Macro-Recovery (1+ days, weekly/monthly)

- Complete digital detox periods

- Time in nature

- Pursuit of non-productive hobbies and play

- Change of environment (even small trips create psychological distance)

The key is proactively scheduling recovery rather than waiting until you're already depleted. Block these periods in your calendar as non-negotiable appointments with yourself.

3. Physical Stress Regulation

The mind-body connection works both ways—physical interventions can rapidly change your mental state. These approaches directly influence your nervous system, shifting from sympathetic (fight-or-flight) to parasympathetic (rest-and-digest) activation.

EXERCISE: The 90-Second Stress Reset

This practice can be done anywhere, anytime you feel stressed or overwhelmed:

1. **Step 1: Physiological Sigh** (30 seconds)

   o   Take a deep inhale through your nose

   o   Take a second inhale to fill your lungs completely

   o   Exhale slowly through your mouth

   o   Repeat 3-5 times

2. **Step 2: Havening Touch** (30 seconds)

   o   Cross your arms over your chest

   o   Gently stroke your arms from shoulders to elbows

   o   This activates delta waves in the brain, reducing stress hormones

3. **Step 3: Cognitive Reset** (30 seconds)

   o   Ask yourself: "What is the next right action I can take?"

   o   Focus on one small, specific step forward

This sequence works by interrupting the stress cycle physiologically and then redirecting your focus toward constructive action.

4. Productive Stress Channeling

Stress creates energy that can be destructive or constructive, depending on how you channel it. Elite performers learn to direct stress energy toward problem-solving and growth rather than worry and rumination.

ACTION STEP: The Stress-to-Strength Redirection

When feeling stressed or anxious:

1. **Identify the Energy**: Notice the heightened energy in your body without judging it

2. **Name the Core Concern**: Ask "What exactly am I concerned about here?" to clarify the specific issue

3. **Assess Control Factors**: Sort aspects of the situation into three categories:

   o   What you have direct control over

   o   What you have influence over

   o   What is beyond your control

4. **Channel the Energy**: Direct your stress energy toward the aspects you can control or influence:

   o   Create a specific action plan

   o   Set a timer and work intensely on the solution for a defined period

   o   Use physical movement to process energy that can't be channeled mentally

This approach transforms stress from an obstacle into fuel for productive action.

5. Stress Inoculation Training

Developed by psychologist Donald Meichenbaum, stress inoculation training is like a vaccine against stress—it exposes you to manageable amounts of stress to build resilience for larger challenges.

EXERCISE: The Gradual Stress Exposure Ladder

Build your stress resilience through controlled exposure:

1. **Identify a Stressor**: Choose something that causes moderate anxiety but is manageable

2. **Create a Ladder**: Break it down into 5-7 levels of increasing challenge

3. **Prepare Coping Strategies**: Select specific techniques for managing discomfort (breathing, reframing, etc.)

4. **Systematic Exposure**: Begin with the lowest level, using your coping strategies

5. **Progress Gradually**: Move to the next level only when the current one feels manageable

6. **Reflect and Reinforce**: After each exposure, note what you learned and how you handled it

Example ladder for public speaking anxiety: Speaking in front of a mirror → Recording yourself → Speaking to one supportive friend → Small group of friends → Larger group → Formal presentation

Overcoming Anxiety and Overthinking

Now let's explore specific strategies for managing anxiety and breaking free from overthinking patterns:

1. Cognitive Defusion

Developed within Acceptance and Commitment Therapy (ACT), cognitive defusion techniques help you create distance from anxious thoughts rather than being consumed by them.

EXERCISE: The Thought Observation Practice

This practice helps separate yourself from anxious thoughts:

1. Notice when you're caught in anxious thinking or overthinking

2. Mentally take a step back and observe the thought as if from a distance

3. Use one of these defusion techniques:

    - **Labeling**: "I'm having the thought that..." (adds distance)

    - **Thanking your mind**: "Thanks, mind, for that thought" (creates perspective)

    - **Visualization**: Imagine the thought as leaves floating down a stream or clouds passing in the sky

    - **Voice alteration**: Repeat the thought in a silly voice or character voice

4. Return your attention to the present moment and what matters right now

This practice doesn't eliminate anxious thoughts but changes your relationship with them, reducing their power to control your actions.

2. The Worry Efficiency Protocol

Not all worry is unproductive—some worry helps us identify and solve potential problems. The key is making your worry time-limited and solution-focused.

ACTION STEP: Scheduled Worry Practice

Transform unproductive worry into constructive problem-solving:

1. **Designate Worry Time**: Schedule 15-20 minutes daily as your official "worry period"

2. **Postpone Worries**: When worries arise outside this time, note them briefly and postpone them to your scheduled period

3. **During Worry Time**:

   o   Write down all your concerns without censoring

   o   For each worry, assess: "Is this within my control?" and "Can I take action on this?"

   o   For actionable worries, create a specific plan

   o   For non-actionable worries, practice acceptance techniques

4. **Limit to Allotted Time**: When your worry period ends, engage in a transitional activity to shift your mental state

This approach bounds worry to a specific time period, making it less likely to dominate your entire day.

3. Overthinking Circuit Breakers

Overthinking creates repetitive thought loops that consume mental energy without producing solutions. These practices interrupt those unproductive cycles.

EXERCISE: The 3-2-1 Pattern Interrupt

When caught in an overthinking spiral:

1. **3 Facts**: Name three objective, observable facts about the situation (not interpretations or predictions)

2. **2 Options**: Identify two possible constructive actions you could take

3. **1 Step**: Choose one small, specific action to take immediately

This technique grounds you in reality rather than speculation and moves you from thinking to action.

EXERCISE: The Mental File Cabinet

For thoughts that keep returning despite not being actionable now:

1. Visualize a file cabinet in your mind

2. Create a detailed mental image of writing the thought on a paper

3. Place the paper in a specific folder in the cabinet

4. Close the drawer, knowing you can retrieve it when needed

5. Set a specific time when you'll review that "file" if necessary

This technique gives your mind permission to let go of the thought temporarily, knowing it's safely stored for later consideration.

4. Uncertainty Tolerance Building

Much anxiety and overthinking stems from discomfort with uncertainty. Building your capacity to function effectively amid uncertainty is a crucial skill in today's rapidly changing world.

ACTION STEP: The Uncertainty Expansion Practice

Gradually increase your comfort with uncertainty through these practices:

1. **Small Daily Uncertainties**: Intentionally introduce minor uncertainties into your routine:

   o Take a different route to work

   o Try a new food or restaurant without researching it first

   o Attend an event where you don't know the full agenda

2. **Information Diet Adjustment**: Practice making decisions with "good enough" rather than "complete" information:

o   Limit research time on decisions by setting a timer

o   Make some decisions more quickly than feels comfortable

o   Identify when additional information brings diminishing returns

3. **Uncertainty Reflection**: Regularly reflect on past uncertainties that resolved well:

o   List situations where you worried about uncertainty but things worked out

o   Remember times when unexpected developments led to positive outcomes

o   Acknowledge your capacity to adapt to unpredictable circumstances

The goal isn't to eliminate the discomfort of uncertainty but to build confidence in your ability to navigate it successfully.

5. Biological Anxiety Management

Anxiety has strong biological components. These approaches directly address the physiological aspects of anxiety:

- **Vagus Nerve Stimulation**: Practices like gargling, humming, or cold water face immersion activate the parasympathetic nervous system

- **Exercise**: Regular physical activity reduces anxiety sensitivity and improves stress resilience

- **Sleep Optimization**: Sleep deprivation amplifies anxiety by up to 30% according to UC Berkeley research

- **Nutritional Approaches**: Reducing caffeine, alcohol, and sugar while increasing omega-3s, magnesium, and B vitamins supports anxiety management

- **Breath Regulation**: Practices like extended exhale breathing (where the exhale is longer than the inhale) shift the nervous system toward relaxation

CASE STUDY: From Anxiety to Advantage

Elena, a marketing executive, struggled with debilitating anxiety before presentations and important meetings. Her overthinking consumed hours of preparation time and still left her feeling unprepared and anxious.

After learning about productive anxiety channeling, she implemented three key practices: the physiological sigh before meetings, cognitive reframing of her anxiety as "performance energy," and the 3-2-1 pattern interrupt technique when caught in overthinking loops.

Within two months, she not only managed her anxiety but began to use that energy as an asset. She channeled her detailed thinking into more thorough preparation, and her heightened awareness during presentations made her more responsive to audience reactions.

Her colleagues began to notice her improved performance, with her manager commenting that she seemed "more present and confident." Elena's key insight: "I stopped trying to eliminate my anxiety and instead learned to direct that energy productively. The same energy that used to paralyze me now fuels my best work."

Key Takeaways: Overcoming Stress, Anxiety & Overthinking

1. Stress, anxiety, and overthinking are not inherently problematic—they become issues when mismanaged

2. How you think about stress significantly impacts its physiological effects on your body

3. Recovery practices are as important as performance strategies for long-term success

4. Physical interventions (breathing, movement, touch) can rapidly shift mental states

5. Building tolerance for uncertainty and discomfort expands your capacity for growth and success

"The greatest weapon against stress is our ability to choose one thought over another."
— William James

In this section on health, we've covered the essential foundations for peak performance: physical energy, mental fitness, daily practices, and overcoming stress and anxiety. With these elements in place, you have the fundamental resources needed to pursue success in all other areas of life.

In the next section, we'll explore Part 3: Wealth – Achieving Financial Freedom, where we'll apply this same systematic approach to building financial success and independence.

3. Wealth: Achieving Financial Freedom

Money is not just about wealth; it's about the freedom to make choices that align with your deepest values. This section will guide you through transforming your financial life - from mindset shifts learned from millionaires to creating multiple streams of income that can eventually lead to true financial freedom.

In the previous chapter, we established that optimal health forms the foundation of success. Now, we'll build upon that foundation by exploring how financial abundance can remove limitations and unlock possibilities in every area of your life.

3.1 Money Mindset: Lessons from Millionaires

Your relationship with money begins in your mind. The wealthiest people in the world don't just have different bank accounts—they have fundamentally different beliefs about money, wealth, and possibility.

The Rich Think Differently

When I was growing up, I had a simple view of money: you work hard at a job, you get paid, and you spend what you earn. This is how most people think. But after studying the habits and mindsets of over 50 self-made millionaires, I discovered something remarkable: wealthy people don't think about money the same way as everyone else.

Brian Tracy, one of the world's leading authorities on success psychology, puts it this way: "Money is a result, a symbol, a reflection of the value you're creating in the world." This perspective represents a fundamental shift from seeing money as something you trade time for to seeing it as something that flows to you based on the value you provide.

"Poor people work for money. Rich people have money work for them." — Robert Kiyosaki

Let's explore the key mindset differences between those who struggle financially and those who achieve abundance:

1. Scarcity vs. Abundance Thinking

People with a scarcity mindset believe there's only so much money to go around. They think, "If someone else gets rich, that means less for me." This zero-sum thinking leads to fear, anxiety, and poor financial decisions.

In contrast, millionaires operate from an abundance mindset. They understand that wealth can be created, not just acquired. They see opportunities everywhere and believe there's more than enough for everyone who provides value.

2. Employee vs. Entrepreneur Mentality

Most people are conditioned to think like employees: trading time for money, seeking stability, and avoiding risks. The wealthy think like entrepreneurs: creating systems that generate money without their direct involvement, embracing calculated risks, and focusing on solving problems at scale.

Even if you work a regular job, you can adopt an entrepreneurial mindset by asking: "How can I provide more value? How can I solve bigger problems? How can I serve more people?"

3. Expense vs. Investment Thinking

Those who struggle financially see most purchases as expenses. The wealthy categorize spending differently - they constantly ask, "Is this an expense that diminishes my wealth, or an investment that will grow it?"

A course that teaches you a valuable skill is an investment. A designer handbag is typically an expense. Wealthy people maximize investments and minimize expenses.

EXERCISE: Identify Your Money Beliefs

Take a moment to examine your current beliefs about money by completing these sentences:

1. Money is...

2. Rich people are...

3. My biggest fear about money is...

4. If I had a million dollars, I would...

5. Making money is...

Now, review your answers. Are they empowering or limiting? Where did these beliefs come from? Which ones would you like to change?

Developing a Millionaire Mindset

Changing your money mindset doesn't happen overnight, but these practical strategies can accelerate your transformation:

1. Cultivate Financial Gratitude

Start appreciating the money you already have. Every morning, express gratitude for your current financial blessings, no matter how small. This practice shifts your focus from scarcity to abundance and primes your mind to recognize financial opportunities.

2. Upgrade Your Financial Education

The wealthy invest heavily in understanding money. Make learning about personal finance, investing, and business a priority. Read books like "Rich Dad Poor Dad" by Robert Kiyosaki, "Think and Grow Rich" by Napoleon Hill, and "The Psychology of Money" by Morgan Housel.

3. Mind Your Money Language

The words you use reflect and reinforce your beliefs. Eliminate phrases like "I can't afford it" and replace them with "How can I afford it?" This simple shift moves you from dead-end thinking to creative problem-solving.

4. Surround Yourself with Financial Success

Jim Rohn famously said, "You are the average of the five people you spend the most time with." This applies especially to financial thinking. Join investment clubs, entrepreneurial communities, or mastermind groups where money conversations are positive and growth-oriented.

CASE STUDY: Sarah's Mindset Transformation

Sarah, a school teacher from Bangalore, always struggled with money despite earning a decent salary. After attending a financial mindset workshop, she realized she was subconsciously sabotaging her finances due to beliefs she'd inherited from her parents.

She began consciously changing her money self-talk, started a simple investment plan, and devoted 20 minutes daily to financial education. Within two years, she had cleared her debts, built an emergency fund, and started a tutoring side business that eventually doubled her income.

Sarah's key insight: "I realized I wasn't just bad with money—I had a mindset that made me uncomfortable with having more than just enough. Once I addressed that belief, everything changed."

Money Blocks and How to Overcome Them

Most people have subconscious barriers to wealth, called "money blocks." These psychological barriers can prevent financial growth even when you're doing everything else right. Here are common money blocks and strategies to overcome them:

1. "Money Is the Root of All Evil"

This misquoted saying has damaged countless financial futures. The actual quote is "The love of money is the root of all kinds of evil." Money itself is neutral—a tool that amplifies whoever uses it. Good people with money do more good; it's that simple.

Solution: Reframe money as a tool for positive impact. List all the good you could do with greater financial resources.

2. "I Don't Deserve to Be Wealthy"

Many people unconsciously believe they haven't earned the right to prosperity, often due to childhood programming or past mistakes.

Solution: Practice affirmations like "I deserve abundance" daily. More importantly, focus on the value you provide to others—when you truly serve, you deserve to be rewarded.

3. "Wanting More Money Is Greedy"

This block often affects generous, kind-hearted people who mistakenly equate ambition with selfishness.

Solution: Define a clear purpose for your wealth that includes helping others. When your financial goals are tied to impact beyond yourself, ambition becomes a virtue, not a vice.

3.2 Creating Multiple Income Streams

The average millionaire has seven streams of income. This isn't coincidence—it's strategy. Multiple income streams provide stability, growth potential, and the shortest path to financial freedom.

Why One Income Source Is Risky

If the COVID-19 pandemic taught us anything, it's that relying on a single source of income is increasingly dangerous in today's volatile economy. Companies can downsize, industries can transform, and unexpected global events can disrupt your primary income source overnight.

Beyond security, multiple income streams accelerate wealth building. When you have money coming in from different sources, you can invest more, take calculated risks, and compound your growth faster than those dependent on a single paycheck.

The Seven Income Streams

Let's explore the main types of income streams you can develop, starting with the most accessible and moving toward those that require more upfront investment:

1. Earned Income

This is money from your job or active business—trading time for money. It's where most people start and often remains a foundation while building other streams.

How to maximize it: Develop in-demand skills that command premium compensation. Negotiate raises strategically. Consider specialized training that sets you apart from peers.

2. Profit Income

This comes from buying and selling products or services for more than they cost you. This includes traditional business profits, e-commerce, dropshipping, or arbitrage activities.

How to build it: Start small with a side business that leverages your existing knowledge. Begin with products or services that don't require significant inventory or upfront investment.

3. Interest Income

Earned by lending your money to others, typically through savings accounts, fixed deposits, bonds, peer-to-peer lending, or financing arrangements.

How to grow it: Start with safe, high-yield savings accounts and fixed deposits. As your financial education improves, explore corporate bonds or peer-to-peer lending platforms with higher returns.

4. Dividend Income

Payments received as a shareholder in profitable companies. Many established companies share a portion of profits with stockholders on a regular basis.

How to build it: Start investing in blue-chip companies with a history of stable dividends. Reinvest the dividends to buy more shares, creating a compounding effect. Consider dividend-focused mutual funds or ETFs if you're new to investing.

5. Rental Income

Money earned by renting assets you own to others. Real estate is the classic example, but you can also rent vehicles, equipment, or even digital assets.

How to create it: Begin by renting out underutilized assets you already own—a spare room, your car when not in use, or equipment gathering dust. Later, you can invest in assets specifically for rental purposes.

6. Capital Gains

Profit from selling investments or assets for more than you paid. This includes appreciated stocks, real estate, collectibles, or businesses.

How to develop it: Educate yourself on value investing principles. Start with small, long-term investments in assets you understand. Improve your ability to recognize undervalued assets in areas matching your expertise.

7. Royalty/Licensing Income

Payment for the use of something you created or own the rights to—books, music, patents, software, or intellectual property.

How to generate it: Identify your creative or intellectual assets that others might pay to use. This could be writing a book, creating music, developing a software tool, or inventing a product that can be licensed to manufacturers.

EXERCISE: Your Multiple Income Streams Plan

Complete this table to map out your income stream development strategy:

Income Stream	Current Status	3-Month Goal	1-Year Goal
Earned Income			
Profit Income			
Interest Income			
Dividend Income			
Rental Income			
Capital Gains			
Royalty/Licensing			

Choose 2-3 streams to focus on initially. Trying to develop all seven simultaneously will spread your efforts too thin.

Strategic Income Stream Development

The key to successfully building multiple income streams is taking a systematic approach rather than randomly pursuing opportunities. Follow these principles:

1. Start With Your Strengths

Your first additional income stream should leverage existing skills, knowledge, or resources. A graphic designer might create and sell templates, a fitness enthusiast could offer personal training, or a good communicator might start a content creation side hustle.

2. Focus on Scalable Streams

Prioritize income streams that can grow without requiring proportionally more of your time. Digital products, investments, and systems-based businesses have higher scaling potential than service-based side hustles.

3. Build One Stream at a Time

Don't try to launch multiple new income sources simultaneously. Master one, systematize it, and then move to the next. This focused approach prevents overwhelm and increases your success rate.

4. Balance Active and Passive Streams

Active income streams (requiring your direct time and effort) typically generate cash faster but cap your earning potential. Passive streams (requiring upfront work but minimal ongoing effort) start slower but have unlimited growth potential. A balanced portfolio includes both types.

CASE STUDY: Rahul's Seven Streams

Rahul started as a software engineer with a single income source. Over eight years, he methodically built multiple streams:

1. **Earned Income:** His primary engineering job

2. **Profit Income:** A niche software tool serving a specific industry

3. **Interest Income:** Strategic investments in high-yield corporate bonds

4. **Dividend Income:** A portfolio of stable blue-chip stocks

5. **Rental Income:** A small apartment purchased with savings from his first four years

6. **Capital Gains:** Strategic investments in pre-IPO startups in his field

7. **Royalty Income:** Technical books and online courses teaching specialized skills

Key insight: "I never tried to build two streams simultaneously. Each new stream took 12-18 months of focused effort before it was stable enough for me to shift attention to building the next one."

Common Pitfalls in Creating Multiple Income Streams

As you build additional revenue sources, be aware of these common mistakes:

1. Chasing Too Many Opportunities

The "shiny object syndrome" leads many people to jump between opportunities without giving any single stream the time and focus needed for success. Commit to making each income stream work before moving to the next.

2. Neglecting Tax Planning

Multiple income streams can create complex tax situations. Consult with a tax professional to ensure you're structuring your income efficiently and taking advantage of all legitimate deductions and strategies.

3. Underestimating Time Requirements

Every income stream requires some time investment, even "passive" ones. Be realistic about your available time and energy when planning new income sources.

4. Lack of Systems and Automation

Without proper systems, multiple income streams become overwhelming to manage. Use tools like accounting software, automatic investment plans, and digital dashboards to monitor and manage your growing financial ecosystem.

3.3 Smart Budgeting & Saving

Creating wealth isn't just about earning more—it's about managing what you have effectively. Smart budgeting and strategic saving form the foundation of financial freedom, regardless of your income level.

Beyond Traditional Budgeting: The Freedom-Focused Approach

Most people associate budgeting with restriction and limitation. This negative framing is why so many abandon their budgets within weeks. Instead, I encourage a freedom-focused approach to budgeting that emphasizes choice and opportunity rather than constraint.

In this system, a budget isn't about telling yourself "no"—it's about prioritizing your biggest "yes." It's a strategic spending plan that aligns your resources with your highest values and long-term vision.

The 50-30-20 Foundation

A simple starting point for freedom-focused budgeting is the 50-30-20 rule:

- **50% for Essentials:** Housing, food, transport, utilities, and base-level insurance

- **30% for Lifestyle:** Dining out, entertainment, hobbies, and non-essential purchases

- **20% for Future Freedom:** Savings, investments, debt reduction, and additional income stream development

As your financial situation improves, aim to gradually shift this ratio toward 40-30-30, then 40-20-40, allocating an increasing percentage toward future freedom.

The Four Financial Accounts System

To implement this approach effectively, create a four-account system:

1. **Essentials Account:** For all necessary monthly expenses

2. **Freedom Fund:** Long-term investments and wealth-building activities

3. **Education Account:** For skills, knowledge, and experiences that increase your value

4. **Enjoyment Account:** Guilt-free spending on things that bring you joy

Automate transfers to each account on payday. This system ensures you're building wealth while still enjoying life today—balancing present happiness with future freedom.

EXERCISE: Freedom-Focused Budget Creation

1. Calculate your monthly after-tax income

2. List all essential expenses and total them

3. Calculate what 20% of your income would be for future freedom

4. From the remaining amount, allocate funds between education and enjoyment

5. Set up automatic transfers to separate accounts for each category

If your essentials exceed 50% of your income, identify one expense you can reduce by 5% this month. Continue this process monthly until you reach the 50-30-20 balance.

Smart Saving Strategies

Saving money isn't about deprivation—it's about making strategic decisions that align with your priorities. Here are proven approaches that preserve your quality of life while building your financial future:

1. Automate Your Saving

What happens automatically, happens consistently. Set up automatic transfers to your Freedom Fund on payday—before you have a chance to spend that money. Start with whatever percentage feels comfortable (even if it's just 5%), then increase it by 1% every three months.

2. Use the 24-Hour Rule for Purchases

For any non-essential purchase over ₹2,000, wait 24 hours before buying. This simple pause eliminates impulsive spending while still allowing you to buy things you genuinely value after reflection.

3. Practice Value-Based Spending

Instead of cutting all costs, be strategic. Identify your personal "high-impact categories"—areas where spending significantly improves your quality of life—and your "low-impact categories"—expenses that don't add much value. Cut aggressively in low-impact areas while preserving spending in high-impact ones.

4. Implement the 1% Improvement System

Each month, find one expense category you can optimize by just 1%. This might mean negotiating a better rate on subscriptions, finding a slightly cheaper grocery alternative, or reducing energy consumption. These small improvements compound dramatically over time.

CASE STUDY: Priya's Savings Transformation

Priya, a marketing manager in Mumbai, tried traditional budgeting repeatedly but always abandoned it, feeling restricted. After switching to the freedom-focused approach, she structured her finances using the four-account system:

- Set up automatic transfers of 5% to her Freedom Fund

- Identified dining out as high-impact and premium subscriptions as low-impact

- Continued enjoying restaurant meals but cut three subscriptions she rarely used

- Increased her Freedom Fund contribution by 1% every quarter

Result: After 18 months, Priya was saving 15% of her income without feeling deprived. Her Freedom Fund grew large enough to make her first investment property down payment while maintaining her enjoyment of dining experiences she valued.

Financial Defense: Protection Strategies

Building wealth requires not just offensive tactics (earning and investing) but also defensive strategies that protect what you've built. Here are essential protective measures:

1. Build Your Financial Safety Net

Before aggressive investing, establish an emergency fund covering 3-6 months of essential expenses. This provides stability during income disruptions and prevents you from liquidating long-term investments at inopportune times.

2. Implement Proper Insurance Protection

Insurance isn't an expense—it's wealth protection. Ensure you have:

- **Health insurance** with adequate coverage for major medical events

- **Term life insurance** if you have dependents

- **Disability income insurance** to protect your earning power

- **Property insurance** for significant assets

3. Regular Financial Reviews

Schedule quarterly reviews of your entire financial picture. This helps identify leaks, optimization opportunities, and necessary adjustments before small issues become major problems.

SMART SAVING TIP: The 3-Category Method

Divide your expenses into three categories:

- **Eliminate:** Expenses providing little to no value

- **Reduce:** Necessary expenses that can be optimized

- **Invest:** Expenses that increase your energy, skills, or income potential

Aim to eliminate one expense, reduce three, and make one investment purchase each month.

3.4 How to Start a Side Hustle

A side hustle is more than just extra income—it's a low-risk laboratory for developing entrepreneurial skills, testing business ideas, and building an asset that could eventually replace your primary income. In today's digital economy, starting a side hustle has never been more accessible.

Finding Your Profitable Side Hustle Idea

The best side hustles exist at the intersection of three factors: your skills, market demand, and your passion. Let's explore how to identify opportunities in this sweet spot:

1. Skills Inventory Exercise

Begin by listing your skills in three categories:

- **Professional skills** from your career or education

- **Personal talents** you've developed through hobbies

- **Transferable skills** like communication, organization, or analysis

Don't underestimate abilities you take for granted. Often, your most marketable skills are those that come so naturally you don't consider them special.

2. Market Research: Finding the Demand

Once you have your skills inventory, research where market demand exists. Use these approaches:

- Search freelance platforms like Upwork, Fiverr, or Freelancer for your skill categories

- Check job boards to see what skills companies are hiring for

- Browse social media groups where your target customers gather

- Use Google Trends to identify growing interest in potential niches

3. Passion Analysis

While passion alone doesn't guarantee success, it provides the motivation to persist through challenges. Ask yourself:

- What topics do I find myself reading about voluntarily?

- What activities make me lose track of time?

- What problems do I enjoy solving?

- What industries or communities am I already part of?

EXERCISE: Side Hustle Sweet Spot Finder

Create three overlapping circles labeled Skills, Market Demand, and Passion. In each circle, list 5-7 items. Then look for elements that appear in the overlapping areas between circles. Items in the center (overlapping all three circles) are your strongest side hustle candidates.

10 Proven Side Hustle Models

Here are ten side hustle models that have proven successful for thousands of people, ranging from those requiring minimal startup costs to those with higher initial investments:

1. Freelancing Your Professional Skills

What it is: Offering services related to your professional expertise to clients on a project basis.

Examples: Writing, design, programming, marketing, accounting, consulting, translation

Startup costs: Very low (basic equipment and portfolio website)

Time to first income: Often under 30 days

2. Content Creation

What it is: Creating and monetizing content through various platforms.

Examples: YouTube videos, blogging, podcasting, Instagram marketing

Startup costs: Low to moderate (basic equipment and editing tools)

Time to first income: 3-12 months (typically requires building an audience first)

3. E-commerce

What it is: Selling physical products online through various platforms.

Examples: Dropshipping, Amazon FBA, print-on-demand, handcrafted items on Etsy

Startup costs: Moderate (inventory, platform fees, advertising)

Time to first income: 1-3 months

4. Digital Products

What it is: Creating and selling information or tools in digital format.

Examples: E-books, online courses, templates, printables, apps, software

Startup costs: Low to moderate (creation tools and platform fees)

Time to first income: 2-4 months

5. Service-Based Local Business

What it is: Providing in-person services to local clients.

Examples: Tutoring, personal training, home organization, event planning, pet services

Startup costs: Low (basic equipment and local marketing)

Time to first income: 2-4 weeks

6. Rental Income Streams

What it is: Renting out assets you own or manage.

Examples: Apartment on Airbnb, car on Turo, equipment on Fat Llama

Startup costs: Varies (depends on if you already own the asset)

Time to first income: 1-4 weeks after listing

7. Affiliate Marketing

What it is: Promoting others' products for a commission on sales you generate.

Examples: Amazon Associates, SaaS affiliate programs, course creator partner programs

Startup costs: Low (website and content creation)

Time to first income: 3-6 months (requires building audience and trust)

8. Coaching or Consulting

What it is: Providing expertise and guidance to help clients achieve specific goals.

Examples: Business coaching, life coaching, fitness coaching, financial advising

Startup costs: Low (certification sometimes helpful but not always required)

Time to first income: 1-3 months

9. Subscription Services

What it is: Providing ongoing value through a recurring payment model.

Examples: Membership sites, subscription boxes, premium newsletters, meal prep services

Startup costs: Moderate (platform, content creation, initial inventory)

Time to first income: 2-4 months

10. Buying and Selling (Flipping)

What it is: Purchasing undervalued items and reselling them at a profit.

Examples: Domain flipping, antique restoration, furniture upcycling, retail arbitrage

Startup costs: Varies (initial inventory investment)

Time to first income: 1-4 weeks

CASE STUDY: Amit's Web Design Side Hustle

Amit worked as a corporate graphic designer but felt creatively constrained. After analyzing his skills and market demand, he started a web design side hustle focusing on small businesses in the wellness industry—a passion area for him.

Initial approach:

- Created three sample website designs for his portfolio

- Set up a basic presence on Upwork and a simple website

- Offered discounted rates for first five clients in exchange for testimonials

- Spent 10 hours weekly on the side hustle while maintaining his full-time job

Results: Within six months, Amit was earning ₹30,000 monthly from his side hustle. After 18 months, his side income exceeded his corporate salary, allowing him to resign and grow his business full-time. He now employs three freelancers and serves clients internationally.

From Idea to Implementation: Your 30-Day Launch Plan

Many side hustles never get past the idea stage due to overthinking or perfectionism. This 30-day action plan provides a structured approach to launch your side hustle quickly:

Days 1-3: Validate Your Concept

- Research competitors offering similar services/products

- Identify your unique approach or advantage

- Have conversations with 3-5 potential customers to validate demand

Days 4-7: Define Your Offering

- Create a clear description of your service/product

- Set initial pricing (research competitors to ensure competitiveness)

- Define what's included and what's not

- Create basic terms and policies

Days 8-14: Build Minimum Viable Presence

- Create the simplest professional presence needed (could be a social media profile, marketplace listing, or one-page website)

- Develop a basic logo or visual identity

- Set up payment processing

Days 15-22: Create Sample Work or Portfolio

- Develop examples of your work (if service-based)

- Source initial inventory or create digital products (if product-based)

- Prepare client onboarding materials or product delivery systems

Days 23-30: Launch and First Client Acquisition

- Tell your personal network about your new venture

- Implement 2-3 focused marketing activities (social posts, outreach emails, local flyers)

- Offer special launch pricing or bonuses to incentivize first customers

CAUTION: Common Side Hustle Pitfalls

- **Legal Blindspots:** Check your employment contract for non-compete clauses or restrictions

- **Tax Implications:** Track income and expenses from day one; consult a tax professional

- **Time Management:** Block specific times for your side hustle to prevent burnout

- **Scope Creep:** Start with a narrow, well-defined offering before expanding

3.5 Freedom Through Passive Income

Passive income—money earned with minimal ongoing effort—represents the ultimate financial freedom. While no income is truly 100% passive (all require some setup and maintenance), creating income streams that don't directly trade your time for money is transformative.

Understanding the Passive Income Spectrum

Passive income sources exist on a spectrum from semi-passive to highly passive. Understanding this spectrum helps set realistic expectations:

Semi-Passive Income (Requires Regular Involvement)

- Rental properties requiring management

- Content-based businesses needing regular updates

- E-commerce stores with inventory management

Moderately Passive Income (Periodic Involvement)

- Dividend stock portfolios requiring occasional rebalancing

- Digital products needing updates every few months

- Automated businesses with outsourced operations

Highly Passive Income (Minimal Involvement)

- Index fund investments

- Royalties from intellectual property

- Fully automated digital systems with outsourced maintenance

The trade-off: Generally, the more passive the income source, the more upfront capital or effort required to establish it.

Five Passive Income Models for Beginners

Here are five proven passive income strategies that don't require massive upfront investment:

1. Dividend Investing

How it works: You purchase shares in companies that pay regular dividends to shareholders from their profits.

Getting started:

- Open a brokerage account at a reputable platform

- Research dividend aristocrats (companies with consistent dividend growth over decades)

- Start with dividend-focused ETFs or mutual funds for instant diversification

- Set up automatic dividend reinvestment to compound returns

- Begin with whatever amount you can invest consistently, even if it's just ₹5,000 monthly

Effort level: Highly passive after initial research and setup

Income potential: 3-5% annual yield on invested capital

2. Digital Products Creation

How it works: You create valuable information products once and sell them repeatedly with automated delivery.

Getting started:

- Identify a problem you can solve based on your expertise

- Create a digital solution (e-book, online course, templates, software)

- Set up on platforms like Gumroad, Teachable, or your own website with payment integration

- Create automated marketing systems (email sequences, social content)

- Establish customer service systems that minimize your involvement

Effort level: High initial effort, then moderately passive with periodic updates

Income potential: Unlimited but varies widely based on niche and marketing

3. Affiliate Marketing

How it works: You promote products or services and earn commissions when people purchase through your referral links.

Getting started:

- Choose a niche you're knowledgeable about

- Build a content platform (blog, YouTube channel, Instagram)

- Create helpful content addressing common problems in your niche

- Join affiliate programs for products you genuinely recommend

- Integrate affiliate recommendations naturally within valuable content

Effort level: High initial effort to build audience, then semi-passive

Income potential: Highly variable; successful affiliates can earn ₹50,000 to several lakhs monthly

4. Print-on-Demand Products

How it works: You create designs for products that are manufactured and shipped only when customers order, eliminating inventory risk.

Getting started:

- Sign up with platforms like Printful, Printify, or Merch by Amazon

- Create or commission unique designs with specific audience appeal

- Set up your designs on products (t-shirts, mugs, posters, books)

- Connect to selling platforms (Etsy, Amazon, your own store)

- Drive traffic through targeted marketing

Effort level: Moderate initial setup, then moderately passive with some marketing

Income potential: ₹10,000 to ₹1 lakh+ monthly depending on design popularity and marketing

5. Automated SaaS (Software as a Service)

How it works: You create (or partner with developers to create) a software solution that customers pay for on a subscription basis.

Getting started:

- Identify a specific problem faced by a defined audience

- Develop a minimal viable solution (can start with simple tools or templates)

- Set up subscription billing and automated onboarding

- Implement self-service support systems wherever possible

- Use analytics to improve the product based on usage patterns

Effort level: Very high initial effort, potentially semi-passive after achieving product-market fit

Income potential: Highest of all options, with successful SaaS businesses generating substantial recurring revenue

EXERCISE: Passive Income Project Selection

Use this decision matrix to identify your best passive income opportunity:

Passive Income Type	My Relevant Skills (1-10)	Available Startup Capital	Time I Can Invest Upfront	My Interest Level (1-10)
Dividend Investing				

Digital Products				
Affiliate Marketing				
Print-on-Demand				
Automated SaaS				

Choose the option with the highest combined score across all columns, giving priority to skills and interest.

Building Your Passive Income Portfolio

Creating multiple passive income streams is a journey, not an overnight transformation. Here's a strategic approach to building your portfolio:

1. Start With Active Income Optimization

Before investing heavily in passive income, optimize your current active income. Increase your salary through negotiation or skill development and reduce expenses to maximize available capital for investments.

2. Follow the 5-Year Passive Income Blueprint

- **Year 1:** Build your first passive income stream while maintaining your job

    o Allocate 5-10 hours weekly to developing this income source

    o Reinvest 100% of earnings back into growth

- **Year 2:** Scale your first stream and add a complementary second stream

  - o Create systems to reduce your involvement in the first stream

  - o Begin developing a second stream using knowledge from the first

- **Year 3:** Optimize existing streams and consider a third

  - o Implement advanced automation and possibly outsource management

  - o Begin developing a third stream in a different asset class for diversification

- **Years 4-5:** Passive income expansion and potential off-ramp

  - o Continue expanding and diversifying your passive income portfolio

  - o When passive income reaches 70% of your active income, consider reducing work hours

  - o At 100%+ replacement, consider transitioning to part-time work or full financial independence

CASE STUDY: Meera's Passive Income Journey

Meera worked as a nutritionist at a hospital when she began her passive income journey. Her five-year progression:

- **Year 1:** Created a nutrition e-book and meal planning templates, generating ₹8,000/month by year-end

- **Year 2:** Developed an online course on specialized nutrition topics, increasing total passive income to ₹25,000/month

- **Year 3:** Added affiliate partnerships with health product companies and began investing in dividend stocks using profits

- **Year 4:** Launched a membership site with ongoing nutrition resources, reaching ₹80,000/month in combined passive income

- **Year 5:** Reduced hospital hours to part-time as passive income consistently exceeded ₹1 lakh monthly

Key insight: "The hardest part was the first year when I was working full-time and building content nights and weekends with little immediate return. Once I had systems in place, each new passive income stream became easier to implement."

Common Passive Income Myths

As you embark on your passive income journey, be aware of these common misconceptions:

Myth #1: "Passive Income Requires No Work"

Reality: Passive income typically requires significant upfront work and ongoing maintenance. The "passive" aspect comes from breaking the direct time-for-money connection, not eliminating work entirely.

Myth #2: "You Need a Lot of Money to Generate Passive Income"

Reality: While some passive strategies require capital (like dividend investing), many others (like digital products or affiliate marketing) require mainly time and skill investments. You can start with whatever resources you currently have.

Myth #3: "Once Set Up, Passive Income Never Needs Attention"

Reality: All passive income streams require some monitoring and periodic updates. Markets change, platforms evolve, and competition emerges. Successful passive income earners regularly optimize their systems.

Myth #4: "Passive Income Will Make You Rich Quickly"

Reality: Building substantial passive income typically takes years, not months. The true power comes from compounding and scaling over time as you reinvest earnings and build multiple streams.

FINAL THOUGHT: The Ultimate Goal of Passive Income

The true purpose of passive income isn't just financial gain—it's freedom. When your basic needs are met through income that doesn't require your daily attention, you gain the most precious resource: choice. You can choose how to spend your time, which opportunities to pursue, and how to make your unique contribution to the world.

4. Relationships: Building Your Support System - Completed

Imagine climbing Mount Everest without a Sherpa guide, proper equipment, or a team to support you. The chances of reaching the summit would be slim to none. In the same way, trying to achieve significant success and freedom without the right people around you is an almost impossible task.

Throughout the first three parts of this book, we've explored how to optimize your health, mindset, and financial situation. But there's a critical component that can either accelerate or completely derail your progress: your relationships. As the legendary entrepreneur Jim Rohn famously said, "You are the average of the five people you spend the most time with."

In this part of the book, we'll dive deep into the power of relationships and how to build a support system that propels you forward instead of holding you back. You'll learn not just why relationships matter, but exactly how to cultivate the right ones, maintain balance between different areas of your life, and protect yourself from toxic influences.

The quality of your relationships determines the quality of your life. This is not just inspirational rhetoric—it's backed by decades of research in psychology, neuroscience, and sociology. Studies consistently show that people with strong, positive relationships live longer, achieve more, earn more, and experience greater happiness than those who are isolated or surrounded by negative influences.

But here's the critical insight that most people miss: building powerful relationships isn't about using people or networking just to get ahead. It's about creating genuine connections based on mutual respect, shared values, and authentic care. This part of the book will show you how to do exactly that.

4.1 Your Inner Circle & Why It Matters

When I first met Rajiv, he was struggling to build his online business despite having excellent technical skills and a solid business plan. After several conversations, I realized the issue wasn't his strategy or work ethic—it was the people he surrounded himself with. His closest friends constantly questioned his entrepreneurial dreams, suggested he get a "real job," and subtly undermined his confidence. Within six months of deliberately rebuilding his inner circle with supportive, growth-minded individuals, his business took off.

This story illustrates a fundamental truth: your inner circle—the 5-7 people you interact with most frequently—shapes your reality in ways you might not even realize. They influence your beliefs, habits, opportunities, and even your self-image. Let's explore why your inner circle is the most critical factor in your journey to freedom and success.

The Science Behind Social Influence

Social influence isn't just a motivational concept—it's grounded in solid science. Research from social psychology demonstrates that humans are profoundly influenced by their immediate social environment through multiple mechanisms:

- **Mirroring:** Our brains contain specialized "mirror neurons" that cause us to unconsciously adopt the behaviors, language patterns, and even emotional states of those around us.

- **Social Proof:** We look to others to determine what's acceptable, possible, or desirable, especially when we're uncertain.

- **Belief Contagion:** The beliefs of our close associates literally "infect" our own belief systems through repeated exposure.

- **Ambient Standards:** The average performance and ambition levels of your group become your subconscious "normal."

These mechanisms operate largely below our conscious awareness, making their influence both powerful and difficult to detect. This is why people who change nothing about their habits except their social circle often see dramatic shifts in their results.

"Show me your friends, and I'll show you your future." - John Maxwell

The Five Types of People in Your Life

To assess your current relationships and strategically build your inner circle, it's helpful to understand the five types of people who might be in your life:

1. **Mentors:** People who are ahead of you on the path, who can provide guidance, wisdom, and shortcuts based on their experience.

2. **Peers:** People at a similar level who provide camaraderie, healthy competition, and mutual support.

3. **Mentees:** People you help and guide, who bring fresh perspective and fulfillment through your contribution to their growth.

4. **Anchors:** People who provide emotional stability, unconditional support, and remind you of your core values.

5. **Energy Drainers:** People who consistently diminish your energy, focus, confidence, or standards through their behavior or attitude.

The most successful people intentionally cultivate relationships in the first four categories while minimizing exposure to the fifth. They recognize that relationships are not just happening to them—they are a resource to be consciously developed.

The Inner Circle Inventory

Before you can optimize your relationship environment, you need clarity on your current situation. This exercise will help you map out who truly constitutes your inner circle and evaluate their impact on your life.

Exercise: Inner Circle Audit

Step 1: List the 7-10 people you interact with most frequently (at least weekly).

____

____

____

____

____

____

____

Step 2: For each person, rate from 1-10 their impact on:

Person	Your Energy	Your Ambition	Your Confidence	Your Growth	Total Score

Step 3: Categorize each person as a Mentor, Peer, Mentee, Anchor, or Energy Drainer based on your assessment.

____

____

____

____

Step 4: Reflect on the patterns you notice. Are there categories missing? Is one type dominating? What changes would create a more balanced, supportive inner circle?_

____

____

The Four Quadrants of Relationship Influence

Beyond just categorizing your relationships, it's important to understand how different relationships influence you. John Maxwell's leadership philosophy offers a valuable framework for this analysis:

	High Challenge	Low Challenge
High Support	**Growth Zone** These relationships push you to grow while providing the emotional support to take risks	**Comfort Zone** These relationships make you feel good but don't push you beyond your current capabilities
Low Support	**Stress Zone** These relationships demand performance but offer little encouragement or emotional safety	**Apathy Zone** These relationships neither challenge nor support you, leading to stagnation

The ideal inner circle contains primarily Growth Zone relationships, with a few carefully chosen Comfort Zone relationships for emotional balance. Most strained or unsatisfying relationships fall into the bottom two quadrants.

The Strategic Approach to Relationship Building

Now that you understand the importance of your inner circle, let's examine how to strategically develop it. There are three key approaches:

1. Upgrade Existing Relationships

Sometimes, the issue isn't the people themselves but the nature of your interaction with them. You can transform existing relationships by:

- Changing the context of your interactions (shifting from purely social to growth-oriented activities)

- Communicating your goals and asking for specific support

- Setting boundaries around topics or behaviors that don't serve you

- Deepening the level of conversation beyond surface-level small talk

2. Expand Your Circle Strategically

Identify gaps in your current inner circle and deliberately seek relationships that fill those needs:

- Join communities where your ideal connections naturally gather

- Pursue mentorship from people who embody qualities you aspire to develop

- Contribute value first before expecting benefits

- Develop the mindset and skills that attract high-quality connections

3. Prune With Compassion

Sometimes limiting exposure to certain relationships is necessary for your growth:

- Reduce frequency of interaction without severing ties completely

- Set clear boundaries around specific behaviors or topics

- Shift the relationship's role in your life (e.g., from close friend to occasional acquaintance)

- Practice compassionate distance when necessary

Case Study: Maria's Inner Circle Transformation

Maria was a talented graphic designer who dreamed of starting her own agency. Despite her skills, she struggled with confidence and consistently procrastinated on taking decisive action. The turning point came when she realized her inner circle consisted almost entirely of either Comfort Zone relationships or Energy Drainers.

Her transformation plan had three parts:

1. She joined a mastermind group of entrepreneurial creatives who were already running successful businesses (adding Growth Zone relationships)

2. She had honest conversations with two friends whose negative outlook was affecting her, setting boundaries around complaining and criticism during their time together

3. She began mentoring a college student in design, which reinforced her own expertise and boosted her confidence

Within eight months, Maria had launched her agency and secured three major clients. The most significant change, she reported, wasn't any new skill or strategy—it was the shift in her self-image that came from being surrounded by people who saw her as capable and expected her to succeed.

Digital Relationships: The Hidden Inner Circle

In today's connected world, your inner circle isn't limited to people you see in person. The voices you regularly consume through podcasts, books, social media, and online communities significantly shape your thinking and standards. Consider:

- Which online personalities do you follow most closely?

- Which authors, podcasters, or thought leaders do you consume weekly?

- What type of content dominates your social media feeds?

- Which online communities do you participate in regularly?

These digital influences function as a "virtual inner circle" and should be curated with the same intentionality as your in-person relationships. Just as you wouldn't invite a consistently negative person into your home every day, don't invite destructive voices into your mind through your screens.

Measuring the ROI of Your Relationships

Not all relationships will directly contribute to your growth or goals, nor should they. Some exist primarily for joy, connection, or meaning—all valid purposes. The key is conscious choice about which relationships serve which purposes in your life.

For relationships that are meant to support your growth, consider these indicators of high relationship ROI:

- You consistently feel energized rather than drained after spending time with them

- They hold standards for you that are slightly higher than you might set for yourself

- They provide honest feedback delivered with genuine care for your growth

- They celebrate your wins without jealousy and support you through failures without judgment

- They expose you to new ideas, opportunities, or perspectives that expand your thinking

- They remind you of your capabilities when you forget them yourself

A Word of Caution: Authenticity vs. Calculation

As you become more strategic about your relationships, beware of viewing people as mere instruments for your success. The most powerful relationships are authentic connections between whole human beings who genuinely care about each other's wellbeing.

The approach outlined in this chapter isn't about manipulation or using people, but about:

- Being intentional about where you invest your relational energy

- Seeking mutually beneficial connections where both parties grow

- Setting healthy boundaries around relationships that diminish you

- Creating environments where everyone involved can thrive

Remember: The best relationship builders are genuinely interested in others, deliver value first, and approach connections with authenticity rather than agenda.

Your Inner Circle Action Plan

Based on what you've learned in this chapter, create your 30-day relationship transformation plan:

30-Day Inner Circle Upgrade Plan

Step 1: Identify 2-3 key relationship gaps in your current inner circle:

Step 2: List 2-3 specific relationships you'll invest more in because they support your growth:

Step 3: Identify 1-2 relationships that need boundaries or reduced investment:

Step 4: List 3 specific communities or groups you could join to find growth-oriented connections:

Step 5: Schedule your first specific action for each of the above items:

4.2 How to Build Meaningful Relationships

Understanding the importance of your inner circle is one thing; knowing how to actually build those high-quality relationships is another challenge entirely. Many people recognize they need better connections but struggle with the actual mechanics of creating and deepening relationships, especially as adults when friendship-building feels more complicated than it did in school or college.

In this chapter, we'll explore practical approaches to building genuinely meaningful relationships—the kind that not only support your goals but enrich your life with connection, trust, and mutual growth. These relationships don't happen by accident; they're built through specific mindsets and skills that anyone can develop.

The Relationship Success Pyramid

Meaningful relationships develop in stages, with each stage building on the foundation of the previous one. Understanding this progression helps you assess where your current relationships stand and what's needed to deepen them.

Stage	Foundation	Key Activities
Stage 1: Connection	Initial rapport and interest	Finding common ground, showing genuine curiosity
Stage 2: Knowledge	Understanding of each other	Sharing experiences, learning each other's stories
Stage 3: Trust	Reliability and consistency	Following through, keeping confidences, being authentic

| **Stage4:
Vulnerability** | Emotional safety | Sharing fears and struggles, accepting imperfection |
| **Stage5:
Growth** | Mutual evolution | Challenging each other, supporting goals, evolving together |

Many relationships stall at stage 2 or 3 because people lack the skills or courage to progress further. Let's examine what it takes to move through all five stages to create truly meaningful connections.

The Six Core Skills of Relationship Building

Regardless of your natural temperament or social style, there are six fundamental skills that create the foundation for meaningful relationships. These skills can be learned and developed through practice:

1. Authentic Curiosity

The ability to be genuinely interested in other people is perhaps the most powerful relationship-building tool. As Dale Carnegie observed in his classic "How to Win Friends and Influence People," becoming interested in others is far more effective than trying to make them interested in you.

Exercise: Developing Authentic Curiosity

Replace these common conversational approaches:

Instead of...	Try...
"That reminds me of when I..."	"Tell me more about how you felt when that happened."
Thinking about what to say next while they talk	Listening to understand, then pausing before responding
Asking general questions ("How's work?")	Asking specific, thoughtful questions ("What project are you most excited about right now?")
Changing the subject to something you want to talk about	Following the thread of what interests them, exploring that topic deeper

Challenge: In your next three conversations, count how many questions you ask vs. statements you make. Aim for at least a 2:1 ratio of questions to statements.

2. Vulnerable Authenticity

Meaningful relationships require showing up as your real self, not a polished persona. This doesn't mean sharing everything with everyone, but rather being honest about your thoughts, feelings, and experiences at a level appropriate to the relationship's development.

Research by Dr. Brené Brown shows that vulnerability—contrary to what many fear—actually increases connection and trust when shared appropriately. The key is starting with "level 1" vulnerability (sharing opinions or minor struggles) before progressing to deeper disclosures.

"Vulnerability sounds like truth and feels like courage. Truth and courage aren't always comfortable, but they're never weakness." - Brené Brown

3. Consistent Reliability

Trust is built through consistent small actions over time, not grand gestures. When you do what you say you'll do—whether it's showing up on time, keeping confidences, or following through on commitments—you build a foundation of reliability that allows relationships to deepen.

This skill is particularly important because its absence can undermine all other relationship-building efforts. A single broken confidence or pattern of unreliability can set a relationship back significantly.

4. Empathetic Presence

The ability to be fully present and empathetic—to truly understand another person's perspective and feelings without judgment—creates emotional safety in relationships. This means:

- Listening without planning your response

- Validating emotions even when you might disagree with actions or conclusions

- Setting aside distractions (especially phones and devices) during important conversations

- Picking up on non-verbal cues and emotional subtext

Exercise: The 5-Minute Presence Practice

For five minutes during your next important conversation:

1. Put away all devices completely out of sight

2. Maintain comfortable eye contact

3. Notice three things about the person's emotional state or energy

4. Before responding to what they say, take a breath and paraphrase to confirm understanding: "So what you're saying is..."

5. Ask at least one follow-up question that goes deeper into their perspective before sharing your own

Practice this intentionally until it becomes natural. Even five minutes of complete presence is more meaningful than an hour of distracted interaction.

5. Value Creation

Strong relationships are built on mutual value exchange. This doesn't mean transactional "what can you do for me" thinking, but rather a mindset of consistently contributing to others' lives in meaningful ways.

Value can take many forms:

- **Knowledge value:** Sharing useful information, insights, or expertise

- **Network value:** Connecting people to helpful contacts or resources

- **Support value:** Offering emotional support or practical assistance

- **Recognition value:** Acknowledging others' strengths and contributions

- **Experience value:** Creating memorable shared experiences

6. Conflict Navigation

All meaningful relationships encounter disagreements or tensions. Your ability to navigate these moments with respect and clarity determines whether conflicts strengthen or weaken your connections.

Key conflict navigation skills include:

- Addressing issues directly rather than hinting or avoiding

- Using "I" statements to express feelings without blame

- Focusing on specific behaviors rather than character judgments

- Seeking to understand before being understood

- Working toward solutions rather than proving who's right

The Relationship Acceleration Framework

While relationships naturally take time to develop, you can accelerate their growth through intentional approaches. The following framework, based on research in social psychology and relationship development, helps create conditions for faster, deeper connection:

1. Shared Experiences

Relationships deepen more quickly through shared experiences than through conversation alone. This is why:

- Working on projects together often creates stronger bonds than purely social interactions

- Traveling with someone can advance a relationship more in a week than months of coffee meetings

- Facing challenges together creates stronger connections than sharing only positive experiences

To accelerate relationship development, create opportunities for meaningful shared experiences—especially those that involve:

- Overcoming obstacles together

- Working toward a common goal

- Learning or trying something new together

- Situations requiring mutual trust or vulnerability

2. Contextual Diversity

Relationships that exist in only one context (e.g., only at work or only at the gym) develop more slowly than those that span multiple environments. Seeing someone in different contexts reveals different aspects of their personality and creates more connection points.

To accelerate relationship development, intentionally create context shifts by:

- Suggesting activities in new environments

- Including the person in different social circles

- Connecting around different interests or topics

3. Intentional Disclosure

The famous "36 Questions That Lead to Love" study by psychologist Arthur Aron demonstrated that guided, reciprocal disclosure can rapidly accelerate intimacy between people. While not all relationships need romantic-level closeness, the principle applies to all meaningful connections.

The key is gradually increasing the depth of what you share while maintaining reciprocity—ensuring both people are disclosing at similar levels of vulnerability.

Exercise: Progressive Disclosure Questions

These questions, adapted from Aron's research, can help deepen connection in any relationship. Start with Level 1 questions and progress as comfort allows:

Level 1 (Low Vulnerability)

- What would constitute a perfect day for you?

- What are you grateful for right now?

- What's something you're looking forward to in the coming year?

Level 2 (Moderate Vulnerability)

- What's a belief you held strongly in the past that has since changed?

- If you could change one thing about how you were raised, what would it be?

- What's something you're still trying to figure out about yourself?

Level 3 (Higher Vulnerability)

- What's your biggest fear about your future?

- What's something difficult you're currently working through?

- When have you felt most alone or misunderstood?

Remember: The goal isn't to race through questions but to create genuine conversation. Share your own answers thoughtfully, listen deeply to theirs, and follow interesting threads that emerge naturally.

4. Practical Support Exchange

Offering and receiving help creates stronger bonds than purely social interactions. When you support someone in a tangible way—or allow them to support you—it builds trust and connection more quickly than conversation alone.

Ways to implement this principle include:

- Offering specific, relevant help based on your skills or resources

- Asking for small favors that allow others to contribute to your life

- Creating opportunities for collaboration rather than just socializing

- Following through completely when you offer assistance

Building Connections Across Different Personalities

One of the most valuable aspects of a strong inner circle is diversity of perspective and thought. This often means building relationships with people whose personalities and communication styles differ from your own.

Understanding different personality types can help you bridge these gaps more effectively. While there are many personality frameworks, a simplified approach based on four communication preferences can be immediately useful:

Type	Values	Connection Strategy
Direct/Task-Focused	Efficiency, results, competence	Be clear and specific, respect their time, focus on outcomes
Expressive/Idea-Focused	Innovation, possibilities, the big picture	Share visions and ideas, allow for creative tangents, show enthusiasm
Analytical/Detail-Focused	Accuracy, thoroughness, logical process	Provide data and specifics, respect the need for analysis, be precise
Relational/People-Focused	Harmony, connection, personal impact	Show genuine interest in their life, acknowledge feelings, be warm

The key insight: When building relationships with people different from you, temporarily adapt your communication style to meet them where they're comfortable. This doesn't mean being inauthentic, but rather showing respect for their preferences, especially in early interactions.

Case Study: Alex's Relationship Transformation

Alex, an introverted software developer, realized that his limited network was holding back both his career growth and personal fulfillment. Despite having excellent technical skills, he struggled to build the relationships necessary for advancement and collaboration.

Instead of trying to completely change his personality, Alex implemented a strategic approach:

1. **Scheduled relationship-building time:** He dedicated two hours each week specifically to nurturing connections

2. **Leveraged existing contexts:** Rather than forcing purely social interactions, he joined a coding project where he could build relationships while working on something he enjoyed

3. **Developed specific conversational skills:** He practiced asking follow-up questions and showing genuine interest in others' work

4. **Created value first:** He offered specific help with coding challenges before asking for anything in return

5. **Built one relationship at a time:** Instead of trying to network broadly, he focused on deepening a few key connections each month

Within six months, Alex had built solid relationships with three senior developers who became informal mentors, joined a high-visibility project team through a new connection, and formed two friendships that extended beyond work contexts.

The key to his success wasn't becoming someone different, but applying intentional strategies that worked with his natural style while stretching his comfort zone gradually.

Digital Relationship Building in a Connected World

In today's world, many important relationships begin or develop partially online. Digital relationship-building has its own set of principles and challenges:

1. Choose the Right Platforms

Different digital platforms serve different relationship purposes:

- **Professional platforms** (LinkedIn, industry forums): Best for connection around expertise and career development

- **Community platforms** (Discord, Slack groups): Ideal for building relationships around shared interests or goals

- **Content platforms** (blogs, YouTube, podcasts): Effective for establishing credibility and attracting like-minded connections

- **Messaging apps** (WhatsApp, Telegram): Best for nurturing existing relationships through consistent communication

Focus your energy on platforms where your ideal connections naturally gather, rather than trying to maintain a presence everywhere.

2. Add Unique Value

In digital environments where everyone can broadcast, standing out requires adding specific, meaningful value:

- Share insights from your unique experience or perspective

- Create helpful resources or content that serves the community

- Ask thoughtful questions that advance the conversation

- Connect relevant people or ideas that others might miss

3. Move from Digital to Real Connection

The strongest relationships eventually transcend purely digital interaction. Look for opportunities to:

- Schedule video calls to deepen online connections

- Attend in-person events where online connections will be present

- Create or join meetups for online communities you're part of

- Collaborate on real projects with online connections

Digital Relationship Action Plan

1. Identify your relationship goals:

____

____

2. Choose 1-2 platforms to focus on based on these goals:

____

____

3. Define the specific value you can contribute to these communities:

____

____

4. Create a sustainable engagement schedule (be realistic!):

____

____

5. Set a specific goal for moving digital connections to deeper interaction:

____

____

4.3 Balancing Personal & Professional Life

One of the most common struggles in today's fast-paced world is finding balance between our professional commitments and personal relationships. We often find ourselves sacrificing one for the other—missing family events for work deadlines, or limiting career opportunities to prioritize personal relationships.

But this apparent trade-off is largely a false dichotomy. The most successful and fulfilled people don't choose between personal and professional success—they build lives where these domains strengthen rather than compete with each other. This chapter will show you how.

The Myth of Work-Life Balance

The term "work-life balance" itself creates a problematic framework, implying that:

1. Work and life are separate, opposing forces

2. The goal is equal time allocation between them

3. Balance is a static state that can be achieved once and maintained

A more helpful approach is to think in terms of **work-life integration** or **life harmony**. This perspective recognizes that:

- Work is part of life, not separate from it

- Different life domains need different attention at different times

- The goal is alignment between your values and how you spend your energy

- Balance is dynamic and requires continuous adjustment

"We don't have a work life and a home life, but one life—it's actually all life." - Sheryl Sandberg

The Four Domains of Life Harmony

To create genuine harmony in your life, it's helpful to clearly define the domains that need your attention and care. While traditional models only focus on work versus personal life, a more nuanced approach recognizes four distinct domains:

Domain	Includes	Key Needs
Professional	Career, work projects, professional development, work relationships	Achievement, growth, contribution, financial stability
Relational	Family, close friendships, romantic relationships, community connections	Love, belonging, emotional support, meaningful connection
Personal	Health, personal growth, spirituality, hobbies, recreation	Wellness, fulfillment, identity, enjoyment, meaning
Practical	Home management, finances, logistics, life administration	Security, order, functionality, peace of mind

The goal isn't to give equal time to each domain, but rather to ensure each receives the attention it needs for you to feel fulfilled and functioning well. Some domains naturally require more time than others, and the appropriate distribution will vary based on your life stage, goals, and current priorities.

Life Domains Audit

For each domain, rate your current satisfaction level from 1-10, with 10 being completely satisfied:

Domain	Current Score (1-10)	Desired Score	Gap
Professional			
Relational			
Personal			
Practical			

For the domain with the largest gap, what specific aspects need the most attention?

What one change would make the biggest positive impact in this domain?

The Seven Principles of Life Harmony

Creating harmony between personal and professional domains isn't about finding a perfect formula or system that works for everyone. Rather, it's about applying key principles in ways that fit your unique situation and values. These seven principles, drawn from research and the practices of high-performing individuals who maintain fulfilling personal lives, provide a framework for creating your own approach:

1. Value Clarity

You cannot create harmony if you're unclear about what matters most to you. Many people struggle because they're trying to balance competing expectations from others rather than focusing on their own priorities.

Take time to define your core values and priorities in each life domain. When you're clear about what truly matters, decision-making becomes simpler and boundary-setting becomes more natural.

2. Energy Management Over Time Management

Traditional time management focuses on squeezing more activities into each day. Energy management recognizes that different activities require different types of energy, and your capacity isn't constant throughout the day.

Key practices include:

- Matching high-energy periods with your most demanding tasks

- Scheduling relationship time when you're emotionally available, not depleted

- Creating buffers between activities that require different energy types

- Respecting your natural rhythms rather than fighting against them

3. Strategic Boundaries

Boundaries aren't walls that separate your life domains—they're filters that clarify what belongs where. Effective boundaries are neither rigid nor nonexistent but deliberately designed to protect what matters.

Examples of strategic boundaries include:

- Device-free times or zones to ensure quality connection
- Communication protocols for work during personal time
- Clear agreements with family about work commitments

- Physical separation between work and relaxation spaces

4. Integration Where Beneficial

While boundaries are important, there are also opportunities to intentionally integrate domains in ways that create mutual benefit rather than conflict:

- Including family in appropriate work events

- Building relationships with colleagues that transcend purely professional interaction

- Bringing your authentic self to work rather than maintaining an artificial "work persona"

- Finding work that aligns with personal passions and values

5. Time Blocking and Transitional Rituals

Creating distinct blocks of focused time for different domains—and clear transitions between them—helps prevent the mental "spillover" that often creates stress.

Effective practices include:

- Dedicated focus blocks for deep work without interruption

- Protected time for key relationships with minimal distractions

- Transition rituals that help you mentally shift between domains (e.g., a walk after work before family time)

- Regular planning sessions to organize upcoming time blocks

6. Communication and Expectation Management

Much of the stress around balancing personal and professional commitments comes from unmet or unclear expectations. Proactive, transparent communication with key stakeholders in all life domains can prevent this friction:

- Clearly communicating work constraints to family and friends

- Setting realistic expectations with colleagues and clients

- Negotiating important boundaries with employers

- Regularly checking in with loved ones about how arrangements are working

7. Regular Recalibration

Life harmony isn't a one-time achievement but an ongoing process of adjustment as circumstances and priorities evolve. Scheduling regular reviews of how your current approach is working allows you to make incremental adjustments before small imbalances become major problems.

Life Harmony Planning Template

1. My non-negotiable priorities in each domain:

Professional:

____

Relational:

____

Personal:

____

Practical:

____

2. My energy patterns (when I'm at my best for different activities):

____

3. Boundaries I need to establish or strengthen:

____

4. Potential integration opportunities (where domains can enhance each other):

____

5. Key expectations I need to communicate or renegotiate:

____

6. My ideal weekly rhythm (key time blocks for each domain):

____

Common Life Harmony Challenges and Solutions

Challenge 1: Digital Overwhelm

The constant connectivity of modern life has blurred the lines between work and personal time, creating a state of perpetual partial attention that diminishes effectiveness in all domains.

Solutions:

- Create tech-free zones or times (e.g., no devices in the bedroom, no email after 8pm)

- Use separate devices or accounts for work and personal use when possible

- Implement digital boundaries (turning off notifications, using "do not disturb" modes)

- Schedule specific times for email and messages rather than responding continuously

Challenge 2: Conflicting Expectations

Different people in your life may have incompatible expectations about your availability, priorities, or commitments.

Solutions:

- Clearly communicate your priorities and constraints to all stakeholders

- Negotiate compromises based on the relative importance of different expectations

- Be willing to disappoint people on small matters to be reliable on important ones

- Recognize when others' expectations are unreasonable and set appropriate boundaries

Challenge 3: Guilt and Internal Pressure

Even with external support, many people struggle with internal feelings of guilt or inadequacy when they can't meet all demands perfectly.

Solutions:

- Challenge perfectionist thinking patterns with realistic standards

- Practice self-compassion during inevitable imperfect moments

- Focus on the quality of engagement in each domain rather than quantity of time

- Regularly acknowledge what you are managing well rather than only seeing shortfalls

Challenge 4: Unexpected Disruptions

Even the best systems get disrupted by life events like illness, emergencies, or sudden work demands.

Solutions:

- Build buffer time into your schedule to absorb unexpected demands
- Develop contingency plans for common disruptions
- Create a priority framework for making quick decisions during disruptions

- Practice resilience through acceptance of what can't be controlled

Case Study: Priya's Life Harmony Transformation

Priya, a marketing executive and mother of two, was constantly torn between her growing career responsibilities and her desire to be present for her family. She frequently experienced guilt in both domains—feeling she was letting down colleagues when prioritizing family, and feeling like an absent parent when focusing on work.

Her transformation began when she stopped seeing work and family as competing priorities and instead developed an integrated approach:

1. **Value clarity:** She identified her core values as professional excellence, meaningful family connection, and personal wellbeing—recognizing that all three were non-negotiable

2. **Energy management:** She restructured her schedule to do creative work during her peak morning hours and scheduled important family time when she was emotionally available

3. **Strategic boundaries:** She established clear "work-free zones" (like family dinner and weekend mornings) while also creating protected work blocks

4. **Expectation management:** She had candid conversations with both her boss and family about her commitments and limitations

5. **Integration:** She found ways to blend domains where appropriate, like occasionally bringing her children to suitable work events

The results weren't immediate or perfect, but within three months, Priya reported significantly less stress, more quality engagement in both domains, and an end to the constant guilt that had plagued her. Most importantly, she no longer saw work and family as inherently conflicting parts of her life but as different expressions of her whole self.

Your Life Harmony Action Plan

Creating greater harmony between your personal and professional life doesn't happen by accident. Use this action plan to begin implementing the principles we've discussed:

1. **Conduct a life domain audit** using the exercise provided earlier in this chapter

2. **Identify your biggest pain point** in balancing different life areas

3. **Select one principle** from this chapter that directly addresses that pain point

4. **Implement a specific change** based on that principle for the next 21 days

5. **Evaluate the impact** and adjust as needed

6. **Add additional changes** one at a time rather than attempting a complete overhaul

Remember that life harmony is a continuous practice, not a destination. Small, consistent adjustments over time create dramatic improvements in how your various life domains work together.

4.4 Dealing with Negative People & Energy Drainers

Even with the best relationship strategies, you will inevitably encounter people whose negativity, criticism, or toxic behaviors drain your energy and threaten your progress. These interactions can undermine your confidence, damage your motivation, and distract you from your goals if not managed effectively.

In this chapter, we'll explore how to identify energy-draining relationships and develop strategies to protect yourself without becoming negative yourself. The goal isn't to eliminate all challenging people from your life— which would be neither possible nor desirable—but to develop skills for maintaining your wellbeing and momentum despite their influence.

Recognizing Energy-Draining Relationships

Not all difficult relationships are truly toxic or detrimental. Sometimes temporary conflicts or differences in style create tension that can ultimately lead to growth. The key is distinguishing between relationships that challenge you in healthy ways and those that consistently diminish your energy and wellbeing.

Look for these warning signs of genuinely energy-draining relationships:

Warning Sign	What It Looks Like
Persistent Negativity	Consistent pessimism, finding problems in every solution, dismissing positive perspectives
Victimhood Mentality	Blaming others for problems, refusing to take responsibility, seeing themselves as helpless
Jealousy of Progress	Subtle undermining of achievements, backhanded compliments, competing rather than celebrating

Emotional Vampirism	Demanding emotional support without reciprocity, creating drama that requires constant attention
Chronic Criticism	Frequent judgment of you or others, focusing on flaws rather than strengths, perfectionist standards
Boundary Violations	Disregarding your stated limits, pushing for more than you're comfortable giving, guilt-tripping
Physical Symptoms	Feeling physically tense, exhausted, or anxious before, during, or after interactions

The most reliable indicator is how you feel after spending time with someone. While all relationships have challenging moments, energy-draining relationships leave you consistently feeling depleted, anxious, or negative after interactions.

Understanding the Five Types of Difficult People

Different types of difficult people require different management strategies. Understanding the patterns behind energy-draining behavior helps you respond effectively rather than reactively:

1. The Critic

Critics find fault with everything—your ideas, decisions, and achievements. Their commentary focuses on what's wrong rather than what's right, often under the guise of "just being honest" or "helping you improve."

Core patterns:

- Perfectionism and high standards (often applied more strictly to others than themselves)

- Fear of inadequacy projected outward as judgment

- Black-and-white thinking that misses nuance

2. The Victim

Victims believe the world is against them and take little responsibility for their circumstances. They often seek sympathy and support while rejecting actual solutions or suggestions for change.

Core patterns:

- External locus of control (believing outside forces determine their fate)

- Secondary gain from problem-focused identity

- Resistance to solutions that would require personal responsibility

3. The Controller

Controllers need to dictate how things happen, often micromanaging, giving unsolicited advice, or becoming agitated when others don't follow their approach. They struggle with others' autonomy.

Core patterns:

- Anxiety managed through control of external circumstances

- Difficulty trusting others' competence or judgment

- Self-worth tied to being needed or being right

4. The Drama Magnet

Drama magnets create or amplify conflicts, often sharing private information, triangulating between people, or escalating minor issues into major crises. Their lives seem to be in constant chaos.

Core patterns:

- Emotional intensity mistaken for emotional intimacy

- Attention and significance gained through crisis

- Poor emotional regulation and boundary management

5. The Emotional Vampire

Emotional vampires demand extensive emotional support while offering little in return. Interactions are one-sided, with their needs, problems, and feelings dominating the relationship.

Core patterns:

- Difficulty self-regulating emotions without external support

- Limited awareness of others' emotional needs or boundaries

- Insecurity leading to constant reassurance-seeking

Exercise: Energy Drain Inventory

Identify 2-3 relationships in your life that consistently drain your energy:

Person	Type of Difficult Pattern	How I Feel After Interactions	Current Relationship Context

The Four Response Strategies

When dealing with energy-draining people, you have four primary response strategies available. Different situations and relationships call for different approaches:

1. Transform (Change the Dynamic)

This strategy aims to improve the relationship by changing how you engage with the person. It's most appropriate when:

- The relationship is important or necessary

- The person shows some capacity for growth or change

- You have the emotional bandwidth to engage in the process

Key techniques:

- Setting clear, direct boundaries about specific behaviors

- Providing feedback using non-blaming "I" statements

- Changing the context or activities of your interactions

- Reinforcing positive behaviors while not engaging with negative ones

2. Limit (Manage Exposure)

This strategy reduces your exposure to the person while maintaining the relationship at a different level. It's appropriate when:

- Transformation attempts haven't succeeded

- The relationship has some value but is consistently draining

- Completely ending the relationship is unnecessary or undesirable

Key techniques:

- Reducing frequency of interaction

- Setting time limits for visits or conversations

- Creating conversational boundaries around certain topics

- Involving buffer people in interactions

- Implementing the "grey rock" technique (being neutral and uninteresting)

3. Release (End the Relationship)

This strategy involves ending an optional relationship that consistently harms your wellbeing. It's appropriate when:

- The relationship is consistently toxic despite boundary attempts

- The negative impact significantly outweighs any positive value

- There are no external factors requiring continued connection

Key techniques:

- Direct communication about ending the relationship

- Gradual tapering off of contact (when a clean break isn't necessary)

- Blocking or removing from social media and communication channels

- Processing the emotional aftermath with support

4. Reframe (Change Your Perspective)

This strategy focuses on changing your internal response rather than the external situation. It's appropriate when:

- The relationship cannot be avoided (e.g., certain family or work connections)

- Other strategies have limited effectiveness

- You want to reduce your own suffering regardless of the other person's behavior

Key techniques:

- Practicing compassion for the person's underlying wounds or fears

- Using mindfulness to notice reactions without being controlled by them

- Depersonalizing difficult behavior (recognizing it's about them, not you)

- Finding meaning or growth opportunities in the challenging relationship

Essential Skills for Managing Difficult Relationships

Regardless of which strategy you employ, certain core skills will help you navigate energy-draining relationships more effectively:

1. Emotional Self-Regulation

Your ability to manage your own emotional reactions is your most important defense against energy drain. When you can observe your feelings without being controlled by them, you maintain your power in challenging interactions.

Practice these techniques:

- Pausing before responding when triggered (the 6-second rule)

- Naming your emotions specifically to create distance from them

- Using physical cues (deep breath, relaxed posture) to signal safety to your nervous system

- Having prepared responses for predictable triggers

2. Boundary Setting and Enforcement

Clear boundaries are essential for managing difficult relationships. Many people struggle not with setting boundaries but with consistently enforcing them, especially in the face of pushback.

Effective boundary setting includes:

- Being specific about what is and isn't acceptable

- Stating consequences you're willing to enforce

- Using simple, direct language without over-explaining

- Following through consistently when boundaries are crossed

Boundary Script Template

When someone crosses an important boundary, use this structure:

1. **Name the specific behavior:** "When you criticize my career decisions..."

2. **State your feeling or impact:** "...I feel undermined and frustrated."

3. **Make a clear request:** "I'd like you to stop offering opinions on my career unless I specifically ask for your input."

4. **State the consequence if needed:** "If this continues, I'll need to change the subject or end our conversation when it comes up."

Practice writing a boundary statement for a current situation:

3. Energy Protection Practices

Beyond managing specific interactions, you can develop practices that protect your energy more generally when dealing with difficult people:

- Energy preparation before difficult interactions (visualization, intention setting)

- Energy clearing after interactions (physical movement, nature exposure, meditation)

- Positive relationship buffering (scheduling uplifting connections after draining ones)

- Creating energetic boundaries (imagining a protective shield or filter around yourself)

Case Study: Raj's Transformation with a Difficult Boss

Raj worked under a micromanaging boss who constantly criticized his work, changed requirements without notice, and created a climate of stress for the entire team. As a key position in his career path, quitting wasn't his preferred option.

After identifying his boss as primarily a "Controller" type driven by anxiety and insecurity, Raj implemented a strategic approach:

1. **Reframed his perspective:** He recognized the boss's behavior came from insecurity rather than a personal vendetta, which helped him depersonalize the criticism

2. **Transformed the dynamic:** He began proactively providing updates before being asked and giving his boss visibility into his work process

3. **Set specific boundaries:** He negotiated clear requirements at the beginning of projects and documented all changes

4. **Developed energy protection:** He created a post-work ritual to release stress and scheduled regular calls with a mentor for perspective

Within three months, while his boss's personality hadn't fundamentally changed, Raj's experience had transformed dramatically. He felt more in control, less emotionally reactive, and able to perform well despite the challenging environment. Eventually, his consistent performance led to more trust from his boss and a gradual improvement in their working relationship.

Protecting Your Inner Circle

As we conclude this chapter and this part of the book, remember that your freedom and success depend significantly on protecting the quality of your inner circle. This means not only managing difficult relationships but being intentional about cultivating positive ones.

Make these ongoing commitments to yourself:

1.   Regularly audit your relationships for their energy impact

2.   Invest most heavily in connections that support your growth and wellbeing

3.   Address energy-draining relationships promptly rather than enduring them

4.   Develop your relationship skills as deliberately as you develop professional skills

5.   Remember that the quality of your life is directly tied to the quality of your relationships

In the next part of this book, we'll explore finding work that fulfills you— building on the strong foundation of health, wealth, and relationships we've established so far.

5. Purpose & Career: Finding Work That Fulfills You - Completed

5.1 Discovering Your Unique Purpose

In our journey through life, perhaps no question is more profound than "Why am I here?" Purpose gives meaning to our existence, direction to our efforts, and fulfillment to our achievements. Yet for many, discovering this purpose remains elusive—a distant lighthouse in the fog of daily responsibilities and societal expectations.

I want to share something personal with you: my own journey to finding purpose wasn't a straight line. For years, I pursued what I thought I should want—a prestigious title, financial security, recognition—only to realize that these external markers of success left me feeling hollow when disconnected from deeper meaning. It was only when I began asking different questions that clarity emerged.

The Purpose Paradox

Many of us approach purpose backward. We look outward, searching for something grand and meaningful in the world that will give our lives significance. But purpose often emerges from within, from understanding who we are at our core and what naturally energizes us.

As Robin Sharma wisely notes: "Your purpose in life is to find your purpose and give your whole heart and soul to it." The search itself is part of the journey.

Key Insight: Purpose isn't something you discover once and forever. It evolves as you grow. What gives your life meaning at 25 may differ from what fulfills you at 45. The constant is knowing how to reconnect with your purpose as you evolve.

The Four Elements of Purpose

Purpose isn't a single concept but rather the integration of four essential elements:

1.   Values: The principles that guide your decisions and priorities

2.   Passions: What naturally excites and energizes you

3.   Talents: Your innate and developed abilities

4.   Service: How you contribute to others and the world

When these four elements align, you experience what psychologists call "flow"—a state where time seems to disappear, and you feel fully engaged and alive in what you're doing.

The Ikigai Framework: Finding Your "Reason for Being"

One of the most powerful frameworks for discovering purpose comes from Japanese culture: Ikigai (pronounced "ee-key-guy"), which translates to "reason for being." This concept has helped countless individuals find clarity about their life direction.

The Ikigai framework explores the intersection of four questions:

What you LOVE (Passion)	What the world NEEDS (Mission)
What you are GOOD AT (Profession)	What you can be PAID FOR (Vocation)

When all four areas overlap, you discover your Ikigai—work that feels deeply fulfilling because it engages your passions and talents while providing value to others and supporting your lifestyle.

Exercise: Finding Your Ikigai

Take 30 minutes to contemplate and write your answers to these questions:

1. What activities make you lose track of time? (Passion)

2. What problems in the world deeply concern you? (Mission)

3. What do people consistently say you're good at? (Profession)

4. What services or skills could people reasonably pay you for? (Vocation)

Look for patterns and intersections in your answers. The overlaps between these areas point toward your potential Ikigai.

Moving Beyond "What" to "Who"

Many purpose-seeking exercises focus exclusively on what you do. While activities matter, who you are becoming through your work is equally important.

Jim Collins, in his research on fulfilling careers, discovered that truly purposeful work addresses three questions:

1. What were you born to do? (Your genetic encoding)

2. What can you be best in the world at? (Your potential for excellence)

3. What makes economic sense? (Your sustainable path)

But Collins adds a crucial fourth dimension: Who do you want to become through your work? This question shifts our focus from external achievements to internal growth.

"The purpose of life is not to be happy. It is to be useful, to be honorable, to be compassionate, to have it make some difference that you have lived and lived well." — Ralph Waldo Emerson

Purpose Beyond Career

While this chapter focuses primarily on career purpose, it's worth noting that purpose can be found in multiple domains of life. For some, the deepest sense of purpose comes from parenting, community service, creative expression, or spiritual practice—areas that may complement rather than constitute their paid work.

This perspective frees you from the pressure to find the "perfect job" that fulfills every aspect of your purpose. Instead, you can design a life where different activities satisfy different dimensions of meaning.

Case Study: Maria's Multi-Dimensional Purpose

Maria worked as an accountant—a job that utilized her analytical talents and provided financial stability but didn't satisfy her creative passion or desire to serve others directly. Rather than abandoning her career, she integrated purpose through multiple channels:

• Her accounting career provided financial security and exercised her analytical mind

• She volunteered weekends at a non-profit teaching financial literacy to low-income families

• She expressed her creativity through a small woodworking business she ran in the evenings

Instead of feeling unfulfilled because her job didn't meet all her purpose needs, Maria created a multifaceted life that expressed her full self through different channels.

Overcoming Purpose Blockers

Several common obstacles prevent people from connecting with their purpose:

1. **External Expectations** Many of us inherit dreams from parents, teachers, or society rather than discovering our own. Breaking free requires distinguishing between others' expectations and your authentic desires.

2. Fear of Inadequacy

The thought "Who am I to do something meaningful?" stops many before they start. Remember that purpose doesn't require extraordinary talent—just the willingness to contribute your unique perspective and abilities.

3. Financial Pressure

Immediate financial needs can override longer-term purpose exploration. Consider how you might create space for purpose while meeting your financial responsibilities—perhaps through part-time purpose work, a gradual transition, or finding purpose within your current role.

4. Perfectionism

Waiting to discover your "perfect" purpose can lead to paralysis. Purpose emerges through action and experimentation, not perfect clarity beforehand.

Exercise: Purpose Blockers Inventory

Identify which of these common purpose blockers affect you most strongly:

- External expectations from family, society, or culture

- Fear of inadequacy or imposter syndrome

- Financial constraints or security concerns

- Perfectionism or fear of making the wrong choice

- Lack of exposure to possibilities

- Past disappointments or failures

For your top two blockers, write one specific action you could take this week to begin addressing each one.

The Purpose Discovery Process Finding your purpose isn't a one-time event but an unfolding process. Here's a practical approach based on both ancient wisdom and modern research:

Step 1: Self-Reflection

Begin by examining your life experiences, paying special attention to moments of flow, joy, and meaningful contribution. Ask yourself:

- What activities have I found most energizing and fulfilling?

- When have I felt most alive and engaged?

- What problems or challenges naturally draw my interest?

- What would I do if money were no object?

- What themes or patterns appear across my most meaningful experiences?

Step 2: Skill Assessment

Take inventory of your natural and developed capabilities:

- What skills have I developed through formal education?

- What abilities do I possess that others notice and appreciate?

- What have I learned to do well through life experience?

- What talents seemed to come naturally to me even in childhood?

Step 3: Value Clarification

Identify the principles that matter most to you:

- What causes or issues do I care deeply about?
- What injustices or problems in the world trouble me most?
- What qualities do I most admire in others?
- What principles would I be unwilling to compromise, even for success or profit?

Step 4: Experimentation

Purpose rarely arrives through thinking alone—it emerges through action and experimentation:
- Identify 2-3 potential purpose directions based on your reflection

- Design small, low-risk experiments to explore each direction

- Set a timeframe (30-90 days) to engage in these experiments

- Keep a journal of your experiences, noting energy levels and engagement

- Evaluate which activities feel most aligned with your authentic self

Key Insight

Purpose is often discovered backward, not forward. Start by taking action in areas that interest you, then reflect on what feels most meaningful. As author David Epstein notes, "Don't try to plan out your life and then execute it. It doesn't work that way. Try things, and when you find something that feels right—double down on it."

Step 5: Integration and Refinement

As you gather insights from your experiments:

- Look for patterns across your most energizing experiences

- Draft a purpose statement that captures the essence of your discoveries

- Test this statement against new opportunities and choices

- Refine your understanding as you gain more experience

- Remember that purpose evolves—revisit this process during major life transitions

Worksheet: Purpose Statement Development

Complete these sentence stems to help formulate your purpose statement:

1. I feel most alive when I am

____

2. People benefit from my contribution when I

____

3.   The problems I most want to help solve are

____

4.   The unique perspectives or skills I bring are

____

5.   My purpose might be to

____

Now try to craft a single sentence that integrates these elements into a purpose statement. Don't worry about perfection—this will evolve over time.

Example: "My purpose is to use my analytical mind and communication skills to help people overcome financial anxiety and build sustainable prosperity."

From Purpose to Career Direction

Once you have a clearer sense of purpose, how do you translate this into concrete career decisions? Here are practical steps:

1. Expand Your Options

Most people consider far too few career possibilities. Research shows that people typically explore only 5-10% of the careers that might align with their purpose and skills. Expand your thinking by:

• Researching unconventional careers in fields that interest you

• Interviewing people who do fulfilling work in areas aligned with your purpose

• Exploring combined career paths that integrate multiple interests

• Considering non-traditional work arrangements (freelance, remote, portfolio careers)

2. Look for Purpose Within Current Work

Before making dramatic changes, explore how you might bring more purpose to your existing role:

- Identify aspects of your current job that align with your purpose

- Seek out projects or responsibilities that engage your values and talents

- Find ways to serve others more directly through your work

- Propose new initiatives that align with both organizational needs and your purpose

3. Create a Purpose-Driven Career Plan

If a bigger transition is needed, develop a strategic approach:

- Set a timeline for your career transition (6 months, 1 year, 3 years)

- Identify skills or credentials you need to develop

- Build relationships in your target field before making the switch

- Create financial reserves to support your transition

- Consider a gradual approach, perhaps starting with volunteering or part-time work

Case Study: Raj's Purpose-Driven Career Transition

Raj worked as a software engineer for 12 years but felt increasingly disconnected from his purpose. Through reflection exercises, he realized his deepest fulfillment came from teaching and mentoring others. Rather than immediately quitting his job, Raj created a 2-year transition plan:

1. Year 1: He volunteered to lead training sessions at his company and taught weekend coding classes for children

2. Meanwhile, he enrolled in a part-time education certification program

3. He built relationships with educational technology companies

4. He saved 30% of his income to create a financial buffer

5. Year 2: He negotiated reduced hours at his engineering job

6. He began part-time work developing curriculum for an ed-tech startup

7. By the end of Year 2, he transitioned fully into educational technology, creating learning systems for computer science education

Today, Raj earns comparable income to his engineering days but feels deeply aligned with his purpose of helping others learn and grow.

When Purpose Seems Elusive

What if, despite your best efforts, a clear sense of purpose remains elusive? Consider these alternative approaches:

1. Focus on Contribution Over Passion

Sometimes we overthink the "passion" element of purpose. Research by Amy Wrzesniewski suggests that in many cases, meaning comes not from following pre-existing passion but from approaching any work with a contribution mindset. Ask not just "What do I love?" but "How can I contribute value here?"

2. Embrace the Multipotentialite Path

Some people, whom Emilie Wapnick calls "multipotentialites," thrive by pursuing multiple interests rather than a single calling. If this describes you, your purpose might be to explore connections between different domains rather than specializing in just one area.

3. Seek Purpose Seasons

Rather than one lifelong purpose, consider that you might have different purpose seasons. For five years, your purpose might center on raising children; the next decade might focus on building a business; later years might emphasize community service or creative expression.

"The meaning of life is to find your gift. The purpose of life is to give it away." — Pablo Picasso

Daily Purpose Practices

Connecting with purpose isn't just about big career decisions but daily mindfulness:

• Begin each day by setting an intention that connects to your larger purpose

• End each day by reflecting on moments that felt purposeful and meaningful

• Practice gratitude for opportunities to express your purpose, however small

• Notice when activities drain versus energize you, and adjust accordingly

• Regularly revisit and refine your purpose statement as you evolve

Exercise: Purpose Integration Calendar

For the next 30 days, schedule at least one small purposeful action each day. These don't need to be major initiatives—just intentional moments that express your values and use your gifts.

Examples:

• Spend 20 minutes mentoring a colleague

• Write one page of your book idea

• Research an issue you care about

• Have a meaningful conversation about ideas that matter to you

• Practice a skill that aligns with your purpose direction

At the end of 30 days, review which activities felt most aligned and energizing. These provide clues to purpose directions worth developing further.

5.2 Career vs Calling – What's the Difference?

We often use the terms "career," "job," and "calling" interchangeably, but these concepts represent fundamentally different relationships to work. Understanding these distinctions can transform how you approach your professional life and help you move toward more fulfilling work.

The Three Levels of Work

Research by organizational psychologists has identified three primary orientations people have toward work:

1. Job Orientation

When you have a job orientation, work is primarily a means to an end—a way to pay bills and support other aspects of life. The core motivation is external rewards (compensation and benefits), and satisfaction comes mainly from what the work provides rather than the work itself.

People with a job orientation tend to:

• Define success in terms of compensation and stability

• Separate their identity from their work ("It's just what I do, not who I am")

• Look forward to weekends and vacations as the "real life" part of their schedule

• Find meaning primarily outside of work—in family, hobbies, or other pursuits

2. Career Orientation

With a career orientation, work becomes a path for advancement, achievement, and increasing influence. The core motivation combines external rewards with the internal satisfaction of progress, status, and recognition.

People with a career orientation tend to:

• Define success in terms of advancement, promotions, and expanded responsibility

• Measure progress against peers and industry benchmarks

• Take pride in professional identity and accomplishments

• Find satisfaction in solving challenging problems and developing expertise

• Invest in professional development and strategic networking

3. Calling Orientation

With a calling orientation, work becomes an expression of your deeper purpose and values. The core motivation is internal fulfillment and the opportunity to contribute meaningfully to something larger than yourself.

People with a calling orientation tend to:

• Define success in terms of impact and alignment with personal values

• See their work as inseparable from their identity and life purpose

• Feel energized rather than drained by their work, even during challenges

• Focus on contribution over advancement or compensation

• Experience a sense that they would do this work even if not paid (though fair compensation still matters)

Key Insight

None of these orientations is inherently better than the others. Many people have perfectly satisfying lives with a job orientation, finding their deepest fulfillment in relationships, hobbies, or other non-work domains. The key is aligning your work orientation with your personal values and life priorities.

The Research on Calling

Studies by psychologist Amy Wrzesniewski found that across occupations—from executives to cleaners—people distribute fairly evenly across these three orientations. Surprisingly, the nature of the work itself doesn't predict whether someone experiences it as a job, career, or calling.

For example, in one study of hospital custodians:

• Some saw their work as "just a job"—cleaning rooms to earn a paycheck

• Others approached it as a career—developing specialized skills and seeking advancement to supervisory roles

• A third group viewed the same work as a calling—seeing themselves as part of the healing team, creating environments that supported patient recovery

This research reveals something profound: a calling often has less to do with what work you do and more with how you approach and frame your work.

How Calling Differs from Career

While careers and callings can overlap, several key distinctions set them apart:

Career Focus	Calling Focus
Advancement and achievement	Meaning and contribution
Extrinsic rewards (status, money, recognition)	Intrinsic rewards (purpose, alignment, fulfillment)
Competition with others	Service to others
Role and title define worth	Impact and expression define worth
Success measured by external standards	Success measured by internal standards
Linear progression up a ladder	Evolving expression of purpose

Case Study: Lisa's Transformation from Career to Calling

Lisa spent fifteen years in marketing, steadily advancing from coordinator to director at a major corporation. She had all the external markers of career success—impressive title, substantial salary, team leadership—yet increasingly felt empty at work.

Through reflection, Lisa realized she had built her career based on others' definitions of success rather than her own. While she enjoyed strategic thinking and creative problem-solving, her true fulfillment came from mentoring team members and seeing them grow.

Rather than leaving marketing entirely, Lisa reframed her role: her calling wasn't marketing itself but developing human potential through the context of marketing. This shift changed everything:

- She restructured her workday to spend more time coaching her team

- She created a mentorship program for junior marketers across the company

- She began teaching marketing at a local college one evening per week

- She prioritized projects that developed new skills in her team members

Lisa still worked in marketing, but her relationship to the work transformed. Her primary identity shifted from "marketing executive" to "developer of human potential," with marketing as her context rather than her core purpose.

Finding Your Calling Within Your Current Work

A common misconception is that finding your calling requires changing careers. While this is sometimes true, many people discover their calling by reframing their relationship to their existing work.

Researchers call this process "job crafting"—reshaping your current role to better align with your calling. Here are three strategies:

1. Task Crafting

Modify the boundaries of your job by taking on more of certain tasks and fewer of others. For example:

• A teacher might develop more experiential learning activities (which she enjoys) while streamlining administrative tasks

• An accountant who loves technology might automate repetitive processes and focus more on systems innovation

• A sales professional who values education might create more robust training materials for clients

2. Relationship Crafting

Reshape who you interact with and how these interactions unfold:

• An IT specialist might establish a mentoring relationship with new team members

• A healthcare administrator might create more opportunities to interact directly with patients

• A designer might build partnerships with sustainability-focused clients

3. Cognitive Crafting

Change how you perceive the purpose and impact of your work:

• A house cleaner might frame their work as "creating environments where families can thrive"

• A financial analyst might see their role as "helping businesses make decisions that create sustainable jobs"

• A retail worker might focus on "being the bright spot in customers' days"

Exercise: Job Crafting Exploration

Analyze your current role through these three lenses:

1. Task Crafting: What tasks could you emphasize, minimize, or modify to better align with your values and strengths?

2. Relationship Crafting: How might you change the quality or quantity of your interactions to create more meaning?

3. Cognitive Crafting: How could you reframe your work to connect it with your deeper values and the impact you want to have?

For each category, list 2-3 specific changes you could implement within the next 30 days.

When You Need a Bigger Change

Sometimes, despite your best efforts at job crafting, your current role or industry simply cannot accommodate your calling. Signs that you may need a more significant change include:

• Persistent misalignment between your core values and your organization's priorities

• Recurring health issues related to work stress

• A nagging sense that you're meant for something fundamentally different

• Envying people in completely different fields rather than those more advanced in your field

• Feeling energized by activities outside work but consistently drained at work

If you recognize these signs, consider a more substantial career shift. However, this doesn't necessarily mean an abrupt change or starting from zero.

The Bridge Strategy for Career Transitions

Rather than making a sudden leap, build a bridge between your current career and your calling:

1. Identify transferable skills that can move with you from your current field to your calling

2. Look for hybrid roles that combine elements of both your established expertise and new direction

3. Conduct informational interviews with people in your target field to understand realistic transition paths

4. Start with side projects that allow you to develop skills and test your interest before committing fully

5. Consider internal transitions within your current organization that move you closer to your calling

Case Study: Miguel's Bridge to a New Calling

Miguel spent ten years in pharmaceutical sales but felt called toward environmental work. Rather than immediately quitting his job (which supported his family), he built a bridge:

1. He volunteered with an environmental non-profit on weekends, developing contacts in the field

2. He requested a transfer to his company's newly formed sustainability division, where he could apply his sales experience to eco-friendly initiatives

3. He enrolled in a part-time environmental management certificate program

4. He began speaking at industry events about sustainable practices in pharmaceuticals

5. After three years of bridge-building, he secured a position with a renewable energy company that valued both his sales expertise and environmental commitment

Miguel's transition took time, but by building a bridge rather than making a leap, he maintained financial stability while moving toward his calling.

The Calling Integration Framework

Whether you're crafting your current job or planning a bigger transition, this four-step framework can help you integrate your calling into your work life:

Step 1: Clarify Your Calling Elements

Identify the core elements that constitute your calling:

- **Purpose:** What impact do you feel called to make?

- **Values:** What principles must be expressed in your work?

- **Strengths:** What abilities naturally energize you when used?

- **Environment:** What working conditions allow you to thrive?

- **People:** What types of individuals do you feel called to serve or work alongside?

Step 2: Assess Current Alignment

Evaluate how well your current work expresses these calling elements:

- Rate each element on a scale of 1-10 for how well it's currently expressed in your work

- Identify which elements are most critical for your fulfillment

- Determine whether the misaligned elements could be addressed within your current role

Step 3: Develop an Integration Strategy

Based on your assessment, choose the most appropriate strategy:

- **Job Crafting:** Reshape your current role to better express your calling

- **Role Shift:** Seek a different position within your current field or organization

- **Bridge Building:** Create a gradual transition to a new field while utilizing existing skills

- **Parallel Path:** Express aspects of your calling through volunteer work or side projects while maintaining your current career

- **Complete Transition:** Make a full career change (typically after testing through other strategies)

Step 4: Create an Action Timeline

Develop a realistic timeline with concrete steps:

- Immediate actions (next 30 days)

- Short-term goals (3-6 months)

- Medium-term milestones (1-2 years)

- Long-term vision (3-5 years)

Finding Calling Beyond Traditional Careers

The future of work increasingly includes non-traditional arrangements that may better accommodate your calling:

1. Portfolio Careers

Rather than a single job, a portfolio career involves multiple part-time roles, projects, or income streams that collectively express different aspects of your calling. For example, someone might combine:

- Part-time consulting in their area of expertise

- Teaching or writing about their field

- Contract work on projects aligned with their values

- Creating and selling products or services independently

2. Social Entrepreneurship

Creating a business specifically designed to address social or environmental problems can be a powerful way to express your calling while also earning a living. This approach combines entrepreneurial skills with purpose-driven impact.

3. Remote and Flexible Work

The growth of remote and flexible work arrangements opens new possibilities for calling-aligned careers without geographic limitations. This might allow you to:

• Work for organizations whose missions deeply resonate with you, regardless of location

• Design a schedule that accommodates your energy patterns and other life priorities

• Reduce commuting time and reallocate it to calling-aligned activities

"Your calling is not something you do for work. It's the person you are becoming and how you show up—no matter what you're doing." — Richard Leider

Exercise: Your Calling Vision Statement

Write a 1-2 paragraph vision statement that describes how your calling will be expressed in your work life 3-5 years from now. Include:

• The impact you're making through your work

• How you spend your typical workday

• The kinds of people you work with and serve

• How your strengths and values are expressed

• How work integrates with other important areas of your life

Write this vision in present tense, as if you're already living it. Read it regularly to keep your calling path front of mind.

5.3 Skill Mastery & Continuous Learning

In today's rapidly evolving world, your ability to master new skills and embrace continuous learning isn't just advantageous—it's essential for long-term success and fulfillment. This section explores how to develop the mindset and strategies for ongoing skill development based on Brian Tracy's Mastery Model and other proven approaches.

The New Reality of Skills

The half-life of professional skills—the time it takes for half of what you know to become obsolete—has shrunk dramatically. According to research from Deloitte, technical skills now have an average half-life of just 2.5 years. This means the knowledge you acquired during education may be significantly outdated within a few years of entering the workforce.

This new reality requires a fundamental shift in how we approach learning:

• From learning as a time-limited phase (education) to learning as a lifelong practice

• From mastering a single domain to developing cross-disciplinary competencies

• From credential-focused learning to skill-focused learning

• From passive consumption of information to active application and experimentation

Key Insight

The most valuable skill in the modern economy isn't any particular technical capability but rather "learning agility"—your ability to quickly acquire and apply new knowledge as circumstances change. People with high learning agility adapt faster, remain relevant longer, and find greater opportunities for meaningful work throughout their careers.

Brian Tracy's Mastery Model

Personal development expert Brian Tracy has developed a widely respected model for skill acquisition and mastery that balances practical application with continuous improvement. The model consists of seven key principles:

1. Clarity

Mastery begins with precisely identifying which skills will create the most value in your chosen domain. This requires:

• Researching the most in-demand and emerging skills in your field

• Identifying skill gaps between your current capabilities and future aspirations

• Distinguishing between foundational skills (which underpin everything else) and specialized skills (which create unique value)

• Understanding which skills complement your existing strengths

2. Competence

Develop basic competence through focused study and deliberate practice. Tracy emphasizes:

• Starting with core fundamentals before advancing to complex applications

• Following the 80/20 rule—identifying the 20% of skills that deliver 80% of results

• Setting specific performance standards for each skill you're developing

• Practicing in short, intense periods rather than lengthy but unfocused sessions

3. Commitment

Make a personal commitment to excellence in your chosen skill areas:

• Decide which skills you'll pursue to the mastery level (vs. which you'll develop to mere competence)

• Establish a regular practice schedule and protect this time rigorously

• Invest in necessary resources, tools, and learning opportunities

• Make public commitments that create positive pressure for follow-through

4. Creativity

Look for innovative ways to apply and combine your developing skills:

• Experiment with applying skills in different contexts

• Combine multiple skills to create unique value propositions

• Question established methods and explore alternative approaches

• Use constraints as catalysts for creative problem-solving

5. Concentration

Focus intensely on one skill area at a time for maximum progress:

• Resist the temptation to develop too many skills simultaneously

• Eliminate distractions during practice sessions

• Use techniques like time-blocking and deep work to enhance focus

• Measure progress to maintain motivation during challenging phases

6. Consistency

Maintain regular practice over time, even after initial enthusiasm fades:

• Establish daily or weekly routines that incorporate skill development

- Track your practice sessions to ensure consistency

- Develop systems that make practice automatic rather than requiring willpower

- Focus on small, manageable daily improvements rather than dramatic breakthroughs

7. Consolidation

Periodically review and integrate what you've learned:

- Schedule regular review sessions to reinforce core principles

- Teach others what you've learned to deepen your understanding

- Connect new skills with your existing knowledge base

- Look for patterns and principles across different skill domains

Case Study: Elena's Skill Mastery Journey

Elena worked in marketing but recognized that data analytics skills would dramatically increase her career options. She applied Tracy's model to develop this new capability:

1. Clarity: She researched the most valuable analytics skills for marketers, identifying SQL, Python, and data visualization as her focus areas

2. Competence: She enrolled in structured online courses for each skill, starting with SQL fundamentals

3. Commitment: She scheduled 5:30-7:00 AM each weekday for skill development before work and told her team about her learning goals

4. Creativity: She sought opportunities to apply her developing skills to actual marketing challenges at work

5. Concentration: She focused exclusively on SQL for three months before adding Python to her learning schedule

6.   Consistency: She maintained her morning routine for 18 months, even during busy periods

7.   Consolidation: She created a digital notebook of key concepts and techniques, reviewing it weekly

Within two years, Elena had developed sufficient analytics expertise to secure a marketing data scientist role, doubling her salary and significantly increasing her job satisfaction.

The Skill Acquisition Curve

Understanding the typical progression of skill development can help you navigate the inevitable challenges and plateaus. Most skills develop through four distinct phases:

1. Unconscious Incompetence

In this initial phase, you don't yet know what you don't know. The skill seems simpler than it actually is, and you may underestimate the learning curve ahead. This phase is characterized by:

• Optimism and excitement about quick progress

• Limited awareness of the skill's complexity

• Tendency to make fundamental errors without recognizing them

• Overconfidence in your ability to advance quickly

2. Conscious Incompetence

As you begin serious study and practice, you become acutely aware of how much you have to learn. This phase often feels discouraging, as you recognize mistakes and limitations. It involves:

• Frustration with slow progress and frequent errors

• Growing appreciation for the skill's subtleties and challenges

• Constant conscious effort required for basic execution

- The temptation to abandon the learning process

3. Conscious Competence

With continued practice, you develop the ability to perform the skill effectively, though it still requires deliberate focus and effort. This phase includes:

- Consistent execution when concentrating fully

- Understanding the principles behind effective performance

- Ability to self-correct errors as they occur

- Still needing to think through each step deliberately

4. Unconscious Competence

Finally, with sufficient practice, the skill becomes internalized and automatic. You can perform at a high level without conscious thought, freeing your attention for higher-order concerns. This mastery phase features:

- Intuitive, fluid performance without deliberate focus

- Ability to adapt the skill to various contexts and challenges

- Capacity to innovate and personalize your approach

- Freedom to focus on subtle refinements or strategic applications

Key Insight

Most people abandon skill development during the "conscious incompetence" phase when progress feels slow and frustration peaks. Recognizing this valley as a normal part of the learning curve—rather than a sign of personal inadequacy—can help you persist through this critical phase.

Strategic Skill Selection

Given limited time and energy, how should you decide which skills to develop? Consider these strategic approaches:

1. The T-Shaped Skill Profile

Experts recommend developing a "T-shaped" skill profile, which combines:

• Deep expertise in one primary domain (the vertical bar of the T)

• Broad competence across several complementary areas (the horizontal bar)

This approach provides both specialized value and adaptability. For example:

• A graphic designer might develop deep expertise in visual communication (vertical) while also building competence in coding, marketing, and user experience (horizontal)

• A financial analyst might master valuation methods (vertical) while developing skills in data visualization, industry-specific knowledge, and communication (horizontal)

2. Skill Stacking

Author Scott Adams popularized the concept of "skill stacking"— combining multiple good (not world-class) skills to create a unique and valuable combination. This approach recognizes that:

• Being in the top 1% of any single skill is extremely difficult

• Being in the top 25% of several complementary skills creates rare combinations

• Unusual skill combinations often lead to distinctive opportunities

For example, someone who is reasonably good (but not exceptional) at writing, data analysis, and public speaking has a valuable combination that few others possess.

3. Future-Focused Skill Development

Anticipating which skills will grow in demand can provide significant advantages. Consider developing capabilities in:

• Human + Machine Collaboration: Skills that complement rather than compete with AI and automation

• Complex Problem Solving: Approaching multi-faceted challenges that require integrative thinking

• Digital Fluency: Understanding emerging technologies sufficiently to leverage them effectively

• Adaptive Thinking: Responding effectively to novel situations and unpredictable challenges

• Cross-Cultural Competence: Working effectively across diverse contexts and perspectives

Exercise: Strategic Skill Assessment

Complete this assessment to identify your most strategic skill development priorities:

1. Expertise Audit: What is (or could be) your primary domain of deep expertise?

2. Complementary Skills: List 3-5 complementary skills that would enhance your primary expertise.

3. Skills Gap Analysis: What capabilities do people in your desired future roles possess that you currently lack?

4. Unique Combination: What unusual skill combination could set you apart in your field?

5. Future Relevance: Which of your current skills are likely to increase in value over the next 5-10 years? Which might become less valuable?

Based on this assessment, identify your top three skill development priorities for the coming year.

Accelerated Learning Techniques

Mastering the process of learning itself can dramatically reduce the time required to develop new skills. These evidence-based techniques can accelerate your progress:

1. Spaced Repetition

Rather than cramming information in extended sessions, space your practice at increasing intervals. Research shows this approach significantly improves long-term retention:

- Review new material within 24 hours of first exposure

- Review again after 3 days

- Review again after 7 days

- Continue with increasingly longer intervals

Digital tools like Anki and RemNote can automate this process for knowledge-based skills.

2. Deliberate Practice

Not all practice is equally effective. Deliberate practice—the approach used by elite performers—involves:

- Focusing on specific, well-defined elements of performance

- Practicing at the edge of your current ability (slight stretch)

- Receiving immediate, actionable feedback

- Making targeted adjustments based on feedback

- Repeating with full concentration

3. Interleaving

Rather than practicing one skill in isolation for extended periods, alternate between related skills. For example:

• A musician learning multiple pieces might practice them in rotation rather than mastering one before starting another

• A programmer might alternate between learning different programming languages or concepts

• A marketer might rotate between practicing copywriting, data analysis, and campaign strategy

Research shows this approach improves your ability to select the right techniques in real-world applications.

4. The Feynman Technique

Named after physicist Richard Feynman, this approach involves explaining concepts in simple terms, as if teaching a child. The process reveals gaps in your understanding and forces conceptual clarity:

1. Choose a concept or skill you're learning

2. Explain it in simple language without jargon

3. Identify areas where your explanation falters or becomes complex

4. Return to your source material to clarify these points

5. Repeat until you can explain the entire concept simply and clearly

5. Immersive Learning Environments

Surround yourself with stimuli related to your target skill:

• Join communities where the skill is regularly discussed and practiced

• Follow experts in the field across various platforms

• Subscribe to relevant publications and podcasts

• Modify your physical environment to support practice (e.g., keeping instruments visible, creating a dedicated workspace)

Case Study: Tomas's Accelerated Language Learning

Tomas needed to learn Portuguese for an international assignment with just four months to prepare. By combining accelerated learning techniques, he achieved conversational fluency within this tight timeframe:

• **Spaced Repetition:** He used Anki flashcards to learn vocabulary, reviewing cards at optimal intervals

• **Deliberate Practice:** He identified pronunciation as his key challenge and focused daily practice on this specific aspect

• **Interleaving:** He alternated between grammar study, vocabulary building, listening comprehension, and speaking practice

• **Feynman Technique:** He practiced explaining Portuguese grammar rules to his partner in simple terms

• **Immersion:** He changed his phone language to Portuguese, watched Brazilian shows with subtitles, and joined an online Portuguese conversation group

While not fully fluent by his departure date, Tomas had developed sufficient language skills to function effectively in his new role and continue learning in context.

Creating Your Continuous Learning System

To maintain skill development as a lifelong practice rather than an occasional effort, create a personal learning system with these components:

1. Learning Goals Pipeline

Maintain three categories of learning goals:

• **Current Focus:** 1-2 skills you're actively developing right now

• **On Deck:** The next 2-3 skills you plan to develop when current goals are complete

• **Future Interests:** A longer list of skills you might explore eventually

Review and update this pipeline quarterly based on changing circumstances and opportunities.

2. Learning Resource Curation

Develop a system for collecting and organizing high-quality learning resources:

• Create a digital database of articles, videos, courses, and books for each skill area

• Follow recognized experts in your target skill domains

• Develop criteria for evaluating learning resources (e.g., practicality, depth, credibility)

• Set aside regular time for resource discovery and organization

3. Practice Scheduling

Establish consistent practice routines:

• Block specific times in your calendar for skill development

• Create different types of practice sessions (e.g., focused technical practice, creative application, review)

• Link practice to existing habits to increase consistency

• Track your practice to maintain accountability

4. Progress Measurement

Develop clear ways to measure advancement in your target skills:

• Create skill assessment rubrics with specific criteria for each level

• Record baseline measurements before beginning deliberate practice

• Schedule regular performance reviews to evaluate progress

• Collect external feedback from mentors or peers

5. Learning Network

Build relationships that support your continuous learning:

• Find accountability partners for shared learning goals

• Join communities of practice related to your target skills

• Identify potential mentors who excel in your areas of interest

• Create opportunities to teach others what you're learning

Exercise: Your Learning System Design

Design your personal continuous learning system by answering these questions:

1. Current Focus: What 1-2 skills will you prioritize developing over the next 90 days?

2. Time Allocation: When specifically will you practice these skills each week?

3. Resource Selection: What books, courses, or other resources will you use?

4. Progress Metrics: How will you measure your advancement in these skills?

5. Support System: Who can provide feedback, accountability, or guidance?

Create a one-page document with your answers and review it weekly to stay on track with your learning goals

5.4 How to Turn Passion into Profession

One of life's greatest achievements is transforming what you love into how you earn a living. This isn't just about following passion blindly—it's about strategically bridging your interests, skills, and market opportunities to create work that's both personally fulfilling and financially sustainable.

This chapter provides a practical roadmap for turning your passions into a profession, whether through entrepreneurship, creative careers, or reimagining your current role.

Beyond "Follow Your Passion"

The advice to "follow your passion" has been both inspiring and misleading. While aligning work with personal interests is powerful, the simplistic version of this advice has several flaws:

- Not all passions translate into viable careers

- Passion often develops through mastery rather than preceding it

- Market needs must be considered alongside personal interests

- Turning something you love into an obligation can sometimes diminish enjoyment

A more nuanced approach involves finding the intersection between:

- What you love (your interests and passions)

- What you're good at (your skills and talents)

- What people will pay for (market demand)

- What the world needs (problems worth solving)

"The sweet spot is where your greatest passion meets the world's greatest need." — Frederick Buechner

The Passion-to-Profession Pathway

Converting passion to profession typically follows a six-stage process. This isn't always linear—you may cycle through these stages multiple times as you refine your approach.

Stage 1: Exploration and Clarification

Begin by deeply exploring your passion to understand its nuances and potential professional applications:

• Identify what specifically energizes you about your passion

• Research different ways people monetize similar interests

• Connect with people who have built careers around this passion

• Experiment with different aspects to find your specific niche

• Consider whether you want this passion to be your primary income or a meaningful side venture

Exercise: Passion Mapping

For a passion you're considering professionalizing, answer these questions:

1. Core Elements: What specifically do you love about this activity or interest?

2. Skill Assessment: Which aspects are you already skilled at? Which need development?

3. Market Research: Who currently pays for services or products related to this passion?

4. Problem Identification: What problems or needs does this passion address?

5. Professional Variations: List at least 10 different ways people make money in this field.

From this analysis, identify 2-3 potential professional directions that most interest you.

Stage 2: Skill Development

Passion alone isn't enough—you need professional-level skills to create value others will pay for:

• Identify the gap between your current skill level and professional standards

• Create a deliberate practice plan for developing necessary capabilities

• Seek mentorship from established professionals in your field

• Consider formal education or certification if relevant to your field

• Develop complementary business skills (marketing, sales, financial management)

Remember that developing professional-level skills takes time—typically 3-5 years of deliberate practice. This doesn't mean you can't start generating income earlier, but recognize that mastery is a long-term investment.

Stage 3: Market Testing

Before fully committing to a passion-based profession, test your concept in the marketplace:

• Create a minimum viable product or service offering

• Identify your potential target market and their specific needs

• Offer your services to a small group of initial clients, possibly at reduced rates

• Gather feedback and iterate on your offering

• Validate that people are truly willing to pay for what you provide

This testing phase is crucial—many passion projects fail not because the individual lacks talent but because they haven't found the right market fit or haven't properly communicated their value proposition.

Stage 4: Business Model Development

With validated market interest, develop a sustainable business model:

• Clarify your unique value proposition—what makes your offering distinctive

• Determine optimal pricing strategy based on market research and value delivery

• Identify your customer acquisition channels

• Create systems for delivering your product or service efficiently

• Develop a financial plan addressing startup costs, ongoing expenses, and revenue projections

Even if you're pursuing employment rather than entrepreneurship, thinking in business model terms helps you articulate your value to potential employers.

Case Study: Jordan's Photography Journey

Jordan loved photography for years as a hobby before deciding to explore professional possibilities. Here's how he navigated the passion-to-profession pathway:

1. Exploration: After researching various photography niches, Jordan realized his passion for architectural photography aligned with his background in design

2. Skill Development: He invested in advanced equipment and technical training, apprenticed with an established architectural photographer, and developed post-processing expertise

3. Market Testing: Jordan offered free photoshoots to three architectural firms in exchange for feedback and testimonials

4. Business Model: Based on market research, he created three service tiers with transparent pricing and specialized in working with mid-sized architecture firms and real estate developers

5. Growth Strategy: Jordan developed a content marketing plan featuring architectural photography tips and industry insights

6. Sustainability: To avoid burnout, he limited client photoshoots to three days weekly, reserved one day for personal creative projects, and implemented systems for efficient client management

Three years after beginning this journey, Jordan's architectural photography business generates more income than his previous design job, with greater flexibility and creative fulfillment.

Stage 5: Growth Strategy

With a viable model established, develop strategies for sustainable growth:

- Create a marketing plan to reach your target audience consistently

- Build systems that allow you to scale beyond trading time for money

- Consider multiple revenue streams to diversify income

- Develop professional networks that create opportunities

- Reinvest in improving your skills and offerings

Stage 6: Sustainability and Evolution

Maintaining passion when it becomes your profession requires intentional practices:

- Establish boundaries to prevent burnout

- Reserve time for pure creativity outside commercial constraints

- Continually evolve your offerings to maintain personal interest

- Create systems that handle routine aspects, freeing you for meaningful work

- Regularly reconnect with why you love this field

Four Pathways to Passion-Based Work

There are multiple ways to integrate passion into your professional life, depending on your goals, risk tolerance, and circumstances:

1. The Side Hustle Approach

Develop your passion project alongside your primary job, gradually building it until it can potentially replace your income:

- **Benefits**: Lower financial risk, time to build skills and audience, clarity about whether you truly want to do this full-time

- **Challenges:** Limited time and energy, slower growth trajectory, competing priorities

- **Best for:** Those with financial responsibilities, people who need time to develop skills, those uncertain about full-time viability

2. The Entrepreneurial Leap

Create a business centered around your passion, either starting from scratch or transitioning after preparation:

- **Benefits**: Full control over vision, unlimited earning potential, complete alignment with your interests

- **Challenges:** Financial uncertainty, need for business skills, responsibility for every aspect

- **Best for:** Self-starters, risk-tolerant individuals, those with business aptitude or resources to access support

3. The Career Pivot

Transition to employment in a field aligned with your passion:

- **Benefits:** Stable income while doing what you love, organizational resources, focus on your passion without business management

• **Challenges:** Less autonomy, potentially competitive job market, organizational constraints

• **Best for:** Those who love their field but don't want to manage a business, people seeking collaborations, those valuing stability

4. The Integrated Approach

Bring elements of your passion into your current role or field:

• **Benefits:** No major career disruption, leveraging established expertise, unique differentiation in your field

• **Challenges:** May not fully satisfy passion, organizational limitations, partial rather than complete alignment

• **Best for**: Those with established careers they don't want to abandon, people whose passions complement their existing work

Exercise: Pathway Selection

Evaluate each pathway for your specific passion by rating these factors from 1-10:

Factor	Side Hustle	Entrepreneurship	Career Pivot	Integration
Financial security				
Alignment with passion				
Growth potential				
Work-life balance				
Work-life balance				
Required skill level				
Timeline to launch				

Add your ratings for each column. The highest total indicates your potentially best pathway, though consider which individual factors matter most to you.

Common Challenges and Solutions

Turning passion into profession comes with predictable challenges. Here's how to address them:

1. The Passion-Profit Tension

Challenge: Commercial requirements can sometimes compromise the elements of your passion you most enjoy.

Solutions:

• Clearly identify which aspects of your passion are non-negotiable vs. flexible

• Create boundaries around creative control in client agreements

• Maintain personal projects that remain purely passion-driven

• Educate clients/employers about your unique approach and its value

• Choose market segments that appreciate your authentic expression

2. Financial Instability

Challenge: Passion-based businesses often have irregular income, especially in early stages.

Solutions:

• Build 6-12 months of living expenses before making a full transition

• Create multiple revenue streams within your passion area

• Develop systems for consistent client acquisition

• Consider subscription or retainer models for predictable income

- Maintain part-time stable work during building phases

3. Market Differentiation

Challenge: Popular passion areas often have significant competition.

Solutions:

- Identify underserved niches within your broader passion area

- Combine your passion with another skill or interest for a unique offering

- Develop a distinctive personal style or methodology

- Focus on specific audience segments with particular needs

- Share your unique story and perspective to stand out from competitors

4. Passion Burnout

Challenge: When passion becomes obligation, it can lose its joy.

Solutions:

- Schedule regular "play time" with your passion without commercial pressure

- Diversify your work to include different aspects of your passion

- Create systems that handle routine aspects you find draining

- Take sabbaticals or creative breaks to renew inspiration

- Connect with community to remind yourself why you love your field

Key Insight

The most sustainable passion-to-profession journeys involve ongoing evolution. Your relationship with your passion will change as you professionalize it. Rather than resisting this change, embrace the evolution as part of your growth. The passion that sustains a decades-long career often looks quite different from the initial spark that started your journey.

Your Passion-to-Profession Action Plan

Based on where you are in your journey, select the appropriate next steps:

For Beginners (Exploration Phase):

1. Identify 2-3 potential passion areas you might want to professionalize

2. For each area, list 10+ ways people currently earn income in this field

3. Interview 3-5 people who have successfully monetized similar passions

4. Experiment with different aspects of your passion to identify your sweet spot

5. Take an honest inventory of your current skill level compared to professionals

For Intermediate (Development Phase):

1. Create a specific 12-month skill development plan for your passion area

2. Develop your unique value proposition—what makes your approach distinctive

3. Begin building a portfolio or body of work demonstrating your capabilities

4. Identify your initial target market and their specific needs

5. Create and test a minimum viable product or service offering

For Advanced (Growth Phase):

1. Refine your business model based on early market feedback

2. Develop systems for consistent client acquisition

3. Create processes that allow you to scale beyond trading time for money

4. Build your professional network and reputation through content or thought leadership

5. Establish practices to maintain passion and prevent burnout

While this ancient wisdom contains truth, perhaps a more accurate modern version might be: "Find work that aligns with what matters most to you, and even the difficult days will feel worthwhile." Turning passion into profession isn't about eliminating challenge—it's about ensuring your efforts contribute to something you genuinely care about.

6. Daily System for a Successful Life

Welcome to the most transformative section of this book. While the previous chapters have provided you with essential insights into the four pillars of success—health, wealth, relationships, and purpose—this section will focus on how to implement these insights into your daily life.

Knowledge without action is merely potential. The difference between those who achieve their dreams and those who don't often comes down to one thing: systems. Not motivation, not willpower, not even passion—but reliable, consistent systems that make success inevitable over time.

As James Clear writes in "Atomic Habits," "You do not rise to the level of your goals. You fall to the level of your systems." This section is all about building those systems—the daily practices, routines, and habits that will transform your life from where it is now to where you want it to be.

Over the next few chapters, we'll explore four critical components of your daily success system:

1. Morning Routine for Success: How to start your day with intention and energy

2. Journaling, Visualization & Self-Talk: Tools to program your mind for success

3. Tracking Progress & Building Accountability: Methods to ensure continuous growth

4. 90-Day Freedom Plan: A blueprint for transforming your life in the next three months

By the end of this section, you'll have a complete daily system that integrates all four life pillars into simple, manageable practices. This isn't about adding more to your already busy life—it's about strategically designing your days to align with your deepest values and most important goals.

Let's begin with the foundation of every successful day: your morning routine.

6.1 Morning Routine for Success

How you start your day determines how you live your day. And how you live your day determines how you live your life.

The most successful people I've studied and worked with—from CEOs to world-class athletes to renowned artists—all share one common trait: they have a deliberate morning routine that sets them up for success. Your morning routine is not just about productivity; it's about taking control of your life before the world tries to take control of you.

The Science of Morning Routines

Our brains are most receptive in the first few hours after waking. This is due to the elevated levels of cortisol—your body's main stress hormone, which regulates energy, metabolism, and alertness. This "cortisol awakening response" provides a natural boost of energy and focus that, when harnessed properly, can be channeled into your most important tasks.

Additionally, willpower has been shown to be a finite resource that depletes throughout the day (a phenomenon known as "ego depletion"). By establishing a morning routine, you're leveraging your peak willpower to build habits that will serve you throughout the day.

"Win the morning, win the day." — Tim Ferriss

The Core Components of a Success-Driven Morning

While everyone's ideal morning routine should be personalized to their goals and preferences, research and experience have shown that the most effective routines contain elements from these five categories:

1. Mindfulness: Practices that center your mind and prepare it for the day (meditation, prayer, gratitude)

2. Movement: Physical activity that energizes your body and clears your mind

3. Meaning: Connection with your deeper purpose and most important goals

4. Mastery: Learning or practicing skills related to your personal or professional growth

5. Maintenance: Self-care practices that support your overall well-being

Let's explore each of these components in detail and look at specific practices you can incorporate into your own morning routine.

1. Mindfulness: Center Your Mind

Beginning your day with mindfulness practices creates mental space and clarity, helping you approach the day with intention rather than reaction.

Meditation (5-20 minutes) Even a brief meditation session can reduce anxiety, improve focus, and increase self-awareness. Start with just 5 minutes of simply observing your breath, and gradually increase the duration as you get more comfortable with the practice.	Gratitude Practice (2-5 minutes) Write down or mentally note 3-5 things you're grateful for. This simple practice has been shown to significantly increase happiness and reduce depression by shifting your focus from what's lacking to what's abundant in your life.
Intention Setting (2-3 minutes) Set a clear intention for how you want to show up today. This could be a quality you want to embody (patience, courage, focus) or a specific approach to challenges you anticipate	Gratitude Practice (2-5 minutes) Write down or mentally note 3-5 things you're grateful for. This simple practice has been shown to significantly increase happiness and reduce depression by shifting your focus from what's lacking to what's abundant in your life.
Intention Setting (2-3 minutes) Set a clear intention for how you want to show up today. This could be a quality you want to embody (patience, courage, focus) or a specific approach to challenges you anticipate.	Breathwork (3-5 minutes) Specific breathing techniques like box breathing (inhale 4, hold 4, exhale 4, hold 4) or alternate nostril breathing can calm your nervous system and increase mental clarity.

Exercise: The 5-Minute Mindfulness Starter

If you're new to mindfulness practices, start with this simple 5-minute routine:

1. Sit comfortably with your back straight and eyes closed (1 minute)

2. Take 10 deep breaths, focusing only on the sensation of breathing (2 minutes)

3. Think of 3 things you're grateful for today (1 minute)

4. Set one intention for how you want to approach the day (1 minute)

2. Movement: Energize Your Body

Physical movement in the morning boosts your metabolism, increases energy levels, improves mood through the release of endorphins, and enhances cognitive function for the rest of the day.

Morning Workout (20-45 minutes) A full exercise session, whether cardio, strength training, or a combination, provides the maximum physical benefit. Research shows that morning exercisers are more consistent and more likely to make it a long-term habit.	Yoga or Stretching (10-20 minutes) Gentle movement that improves flexibility, reduces stiffness, and connects your mind and body. Even 10 minutes of basic stretches can significantly improve how your body feels throughout the day.
Quick Movement Burst (3-7 minutes) Short, intense exercises like jumping jacks, push-ups, squats, or burpees can quickly elevate your heart rate and energy. Even these brief sessions trigger many of the same benefits as longer workouts.	Morning Walk (10-30 minutes) Walking, especially in nature or daylight, helps regulate your circadian rhythm, boosts vitamin D production, and provides gentle movement to start your day. It's also an excellent time for reflection or listening to educational content.

Quick Tip: Movement Stacking

If time is limited, combine movement with other morning activities. Listen to educational podcasts or audiobooks while walking, practice gratitude while stretching, or use workout time for mental rehearsal of your day ahead.

3. Meaning: Connect with Your Purpose

Taking time to connect with your deeper why and your most important goals ensures that you're not just busy, but focused on what truly matters.

Goal Review (5 minutes) Briefly review your short and long-term goals. This reinforces their importance and keeps them top of mind as you make decisions throughout the day. Reading Inspirational Material (5-15 minutes) Reading spiritual texts, philosophy, biographies, or other inspirational material can center you on what matters most and provide wisdom to guide your day.	**Purpose Reflection (3-5 minutes)** **Ask yourself: "How can I serve my purpose today?" or "What would make today meaningful?" This aligns your daily actions with your deeper values and life mi Visualization (3-5 minutes)** **Vividly imagine yourself living your ideal day or achieving your most important goals. This mental rehearsal primes your brain to recognize opportunities and take actions aligned with your vision.ssion.**

Exercise: The Purpose Primer

Take 5 minutes each morning to answer these three questions:

1. What's one thing I could do today that would move me closer to my biggest goal?

2. Who could I help or add value to today?

3. What would make me feel that today was well-lived when I go to bed tonight?

4. Mastery: Grow Your Skills

Dedicating morning time to learning and skill development compounds over time, leading to expertise and creating opportunities for career advancement and personal fulfillment.

Skill Practice (15-45 minutes) Deliberate practice of skills related to your work or passions. This could be writing, coding, language learning, playing an instrument, or any other skill you're developing. Online Learning (15-30 minutes) Courses, tutorials, or educational videos can provide structured learning in virtually any field. Even 15 minutes per day on a platform like Coursera, Skillshare, or YouTube can build valuable skills over time.	Reading (15-30 minutes) Reading books related to your field, personal development, or areas of interest expands your knowledge base and exposes you to new ideas. Just 20 minutes of daily reading can lead to consuming 20+ books per year. Problem Solving (10-20 minutes) Tackling challenging problems or puzzles related to your field sharpens your thinking and deepens your expertise. This could be chess problems, coding challenges, case studies, or creative exercises.

The 1% Rule for Skill Development

Aim to improve just 1% each day in your chosen area. These tiny improvements compound dramatically over time—improving 1% daily for a year means you'll be 37 times better by the end of the year due to compounding effects.

5. Maintenance: Self-Care Practices

Tending to your basic needs ensures you have the physical and emotional resources to thrive throughout the day.

Hydration (1 minute) Nutritious Breakfast (10-20 minutes) Drinking 16-24oz of water first thing in the morning rehydrates your body after sleep, boosts metabolism, and improves cognitive function. Consider adding lemon for additional digestive and immune benefits.	A balanced breakfast with protein, healthy fats, and complex carbohydrates stabilizes blood sugar and provides sustained energy. Preparing a nutritious breakfast is an act of self-care that pays dividends throughout the day.
Journaling (5-15 minutes) Writing down thoughts, ideas, and feelings provides mental clarity, reduces anxiety, and creates a record of your journey. Even a brief journaling session can have significant emotional benefits.	Planning (5-10 minutes) Reviewing your calendar and planning your day's tasks creates structure and reduces decision fatigue. Identifying 1-3 "Most Important Tasks" ensures you focus on high-impact activities

Morning Routines for Different Life Situations

Your morning routine should adapt to your life circumstances while maintaining core elements that support your success. Here are tailored approaches for different situations:

For Busy Parents: The 20-Minute Power Routine

Sarah's Story: As a single mother of two young children, Sarah struggled to find time for herself in the mornings. By waking up just 20 minutes before her kids, she created this streamlined routine:

• 5 minutes: Meditation and gratitude

• 5 minutes: Quick stretching or yoga

• 5 minutes: Goal review and daily planning

• 5 minutes: Hydration and nutritional planning

This brief but intentional routine helped Sarah feel centered and prepared, even on hectic mornings. She found that starting the day with purpose made her more patient with her children and more focused at work.

For Corporate Professionals: The Achievement Accelerator

Michael's Story: As an executive at a technology company, Michael needed mental clarity and strategic focus. His 60-minute morning routine became his competitive advantage:

• 10 minutes: Meditation and breathing exercises

• 20 minutes: High-intensity interval training

• 10 minutes: Reading industry news or business books

• 10 minutes: Strategic planning and priority setting

• 10 minutes: Nutritious breakfast while reviewing daily schedule

This routine helped Michael stay ahead of industry trends, maintain energy for high-stakes meetings, and make strategic decisions rather than just reacting to daily pressures.

For Creative Professionals: The Creativity Cultivator

Elena's Story: As a freelance designer, Elena needed to maintain consistent creative output. Her 90-minute morning routine became the foundation of her creative practice:

• 15 minutes: Meditation and visualization

• 20 minutes: Morning walk or gentle yoga

• 20 minutes: Free writing or sketching (without judgment or purpose)

• 15 minutes: Reading inspiring creative work

• 20 minutes: Planning creative projects and setting daily creative goals

This routine helped Elena overcome creative blocks, generate fresh ideas, and maintain consistent output even when client deadlines created pressure.

For Entrepreneurs: The Visionary Builder

Raj's Story: As the founder of a growing startup, Raj needed both strategic vision and practical execution. His 75-minute routine became crucial to balancing these demands:

• 10 minutes: Meditation and intention setting

• 20 minutes: Strength training or running

• 15 minutes: Reviewing business metrics and goals

• 15 minutes: Strategic thinking about one major business challenge

• 15 minutes: Planning high-leverage activities and delegations

This routine helped Raj stay connected to his company's mission while identifying the most important actions to move the business forward each day.

Building Your Personalized Morning Routine

Now it's time to design your own morning routine. Remember, the perfect routine is one that you'll actually follow consistently and that addresses your specific needs and goals.

Morning Routine Builder Worksheet

Step 1: How much time can you realistically dedicate to your morning routine?

Step 2: What time will you need to wake up to implement this routine?

Step 3: Select 1-2 practices from each category that resonate with you:

Mindfulness practices:

☐ Meditation

☐ Gratitude practice

☐ Intention setting

☐ Breathwork

☐ Other:_____________________________

Movement practices:

☐ Full workout

☐ Yoga/stretching

☐ Quick movement burst

☐ Morning walk

☐ Other: ___________________________

Meaning practices:

☐ Goal review

☐ Purpose reflection

☐ Reading inspirational material

☐ Visualization

☐ Other:_____________________________

Mastery practices:

- [ ] Skill practice
- [ ] Reading
- [ ] Online learning
- [ ] Problem solving
- [ ] Other:_______________________________

Maintenance practices:

- [ ] Hydration
- [ ] Nutritious breakfast
- [ ] Journaling
- [ ] Planning
- [ ] Other:_______________________________

Step 4: Create your routine sequence and timing:

Time	Activity	Duration

Implementing Your Morning Routine: The 30-Day Method

A new morning routine won't stick overnight. The key to making lasting change is starting small, building gradually, and creating the right environment for success.

Phase 1: Preparation (Days 1-3)

• **Set your environment:** Prepare your morning space the night before (workout clothes ready, meditation cushion set up, journal and pen accessible)

• **Eliminate friction:** Remove potential barriers (set multiple alarms, put your phone in another room to avoid morning scrolling)

• **Improve your evening routine:** Go to bed early enough to get sufficient sleep and avoid screen time 30-60 minutes before sleep

Phase 2: Foundation Building (Days 4-10)

• **Start with consistency over duration:** Begin with just 10-15 minutes of your routine, focusing on showing up every day rather than doing the full routine

• **Wake up at the same time:** Set your wake-up time and stick to it, even on weekends

• **Create a trigger:** Establish a simple first action that signals the start of your routine (drinking a glass of water, making your bed, etc.)

Phase 3: Expansion (Days 11-20)

• Gradually increase duration: Add 5-10 minutes every few days as the shorter routine becomes habitual

• Add components: Introduce additional elements of your ideal routine one at a time

• Track your consistency: Use a habit tracker to monitor your adherence and celebrate your wins

Phase 4: Refinement (Days 21-30)

• Assess impact: Notice how different components of your routine affect your energy, mood, and productivity

• Make adjustments: Modify your routine based on what's working best

• Create contingency plans: Develop abbreviated versions of your routine for busy days, travel, or unexpected situations

30-Day Morning Routine Tracker

Day	Wake Up Time	Routine Completed	Energy Level (1-10)	Notes
1				
2				
3				
4				

Continue for all 30 days...

Overcoming Common Morning Routine Challenges

Challenge: "I'm not a morning person"	**Challenge: "I don't have enough time"**
Solution: Shift your circadian rhythm gradually by going to bed and waking up 15 minutes earlier each day. Expose yourself to morning sunlight immediately after waking to reset your body clock. After 2-3 weeks of consistency, your body will adapt.	**Solution:** Start with just 10 minutes and focus on the highest-impact activities. Remember that a morning routine often creates more time through increased productivity and better decision-making throughout the day.
Challenge: "I can't maintain consistency"	**Challenge: "I live with others who disrupt my routine"**

<table>
<tr><td>Solution: Use habit stacking (attaching new habits to existing ones) and environmental design (setting up your space the night before). Focus on showing up daily, even for an abbreviated version of your routine</td><td>Solution: Communicate the importance of your routine to family members. Consider finding a dedicated space, using headphones, or waking up before others. Create a modified routine for days when disruptions are unavoidable.</td></tr>
</table>

The Power of Flexibility

The most sustainable morning routines have both structure and flexibility. Create three versions of your routine:

1. Ideal Routine: When you have full time and energy (30-90 minutes)

2. Essential Routine: The core elements you need most (15-30 minutes)

3. Minimal Routine: The non-negotiable practices for your busiest days (5-15 minutes)

Having these options prevents all-or-nothing thinking and helps maintain consistency through changing life circumstances.

Final Thoughts on Morning Routines

Your morning routine is more than a set of activities—it's a statement about what you value and who you're becoming. By taking control of the first hour of your day, you set in motion a cascade of positive effects that influence everything that follows.

Remember that the goal isn't perfection, but progress. Some mornings will go exactly as planned, while others won't. What matters is the commitment to beginning each day with intention and purpose, consistently moving toward your vision of success.

In the next chapter, we'll explore how journaling, visualization, and self-talk can further accelerate your journey to success by harnessing the power of your mind.

6.2 Journaling, Visualization & Self-Talk

Your success is determined not just by your actions, but by your thoughts. The most powerful tool you have is your mind, and in this chapter, we'll explore three science-backed methods to program your mind for success: journaling, visualization, and self-talk.

These practices are not merely nice-to-have additions to your routine—they are essential tools used by elite performers across every field. From Olympic athletes to billionaire entrepreneurs, those who have reached the highest levels of achievement understand that mental conditioning is just as important as skill development.

The Science of Mind Programming

Before diving into specific techniques, let's understand why these practices work. Our brains are constantly being programmed—the only question is whether you're doing the programming intentionally or allowing external forces to shape your thinking.

Three key neurological principles make these practices so effective:

1. **Neuroplasticity:** Your brain physically rewires itself based on repeated thoughts and experiences. Consistent mental practices create new neural pathways that eventually become automatic.

2. **Reticular Activating System (RAS):** This neural network acts as a filter, determining what information from your environment reaches your conscious awareness. When you consistently focus on specific goals or ideas through journaling and visualization, your RAS begins to notice opportunities and resources related to these focuses that you might otherwise miss.

3. **Cognitive-Behavioral Connection:** Research conclusively shows that changing thought patterns directly affects emotional states and behavior. By deliberately managing your internal dialogue, you influence your feelings and actions.

With this scientific foundation in mind, let's explore each practice in detail.

Journaling: Clarifying Thoughts and Tracking Progress

Journaling is one of the most powerful yet underutilized tools for personal development. Unlike casual diary-keeping, strategic journaling is a structured approach to processing experiences, clarifying thinking, and accelerating growth.

Benefits of Consistent Journaling

- Provides mental clarity and reduces anxiety

- Creates a record of progress and insights

- Strengthens self-awareness and emotional intelligence

- Improves problem-solving abilities through structured thinking

- Enhances goal achievement through accountability and focus

Types of Journaling for Success

| 1. Gratitude Journaling
Recording 3-5 things you're grateful for each day has been shown to significantly increase happiness, reduce depression, and improve physical health. The key is to be specific and focus on why each item matters to you.

Prompt example: "What three things am I truly grateful for today, and why do they matter to me?"

3. Reflection Journaling
Processing your experiences through writing helps extract lessons and identify patterns. This turns everyday experiences into valuable learning opportunities. | 2. Goal-Focused Journaling
Regularly writing about your goals keeps them top of mind and helps you track progress. Studies show that you're 42% more likely to achieve goals that you've written down and reviewed regularly.

Prompt example: "What is my most important goal right now, and what specific action can I take today to move closer to it?"

4. Problem-Solving Journaling
Writing through challenges helps separate emotions from facts and generates solutions you might not see when the problem is just swirling in your head. |

Prompt example: "What went well today? What could have gone better? What did I learn that I can apply tomorrow?"	**Prompt example:** "What exactly is the problem I'm facing? What are all possible solutions? What's the next specific step I can take?"
5. Idea Journaling Capturing insights, inspirations, and creative ideas preserves them for later development and connects concepts that might otherwise remain separate. **Prompt example:** "What new ideas or insights occurred to me today? How might they connect to my current projects or goals?"	6. Habit Tracking Journaling Recording your adherence to key habits provides accountability and helps identify patterns that support or undermine your success. **Prompt example:** "Which of my core habits did I complete today? What made it easy or difficult to follow through?"

Exercise: The 5-Minute Journaling Method

If you're new to journaling or short on time, this simple 5-minute structure provides maximum benefits:

1. Three Gratitude's (1 minute): List three specific things you're grateful for today

2. Daily Intention (1 minute): Write one sentence about how you want to approach the day

3. Top 3 Goals (1 minute): List your three most important tasks or goals for the day

4. Affirmation (1 minute): Write one empowering statement about yourself in the present tense

5. Learning/Insight (1 minute): Note one thing you've recently learned or realized

Advanced Journaling Techniques

Future Self Journaling Write from the perspective of your future self who has already achieved your goals. Describe your daily life, feelings, and accomplishments in vivid detail. This creates a compelling vision that motivates current actions. **Example prompt**: "It's [5 years from now]. Write about a typical day in your life as if you've achieved all your current goals." Value Alignment Journaling Regularly assess how your actions align with your core values. This helps reduce internal conflict and ensures you're building a life that truly feels successful to you. **Example prompt**: "Which of my core values did I honor today? Where did my actions conflict with my values?"	Shadow Work Journaling Explore aspects of yourself that you typically avoid or deny. This type of journaling helps integrate unconscious patterns that may be sabotaging your success. **Example prompt**: "What part of myself am I reluctant to acknowledge? How might this aspect be affecting my goals?" Decision Journaling Record important decisions, including your reasoning, expected outcomes, and uncertainties. Reviewing these entries later improves decision-making by revealing patterns and biases. **Example prompt**: "What important decision am I facing? What factors am I considering? What do I predict will happen?"

Creating a Sustainable Journaling Habit

The most effective journal is the one you'll actually use consistently. Consider these approaches:

• Digital vs. Physical: Choose the format that feels most natural to you—handwritten journals promote deeper processing, while digital journals offer searchability and accessibility

• Time Anchoring: Connect journaling to an existing habit (morning coffee, before bed) to increase consistency

• Prompts: Use prepared prompts (like those in this chapter) to overcome blank page syndrome

• No Perfectionism: Your journal is a tool, not a publication—spelling, grammar, and eloquence don't matter

Visualization: Mental Rehearsal for Success

Visualization is the practice of creating vivid mental images of desired outcomes or performances. Far from mere daydreaming, effective visualization is a disciplined technique used by elite performers to program their minds for success.

The Science Behind Visualization

When you vividly imagine an experience, your brain activates many of the same neural pathways that fire during the actual experience. Research in sports psychology has shown that mental practice activates the same motor cortex regions as physical practice, creating neural patterns that enhance **physical performance.**

Studies across various disciplines demonstrate that visualization:

• Improves physical performance in athletes (some studies show improvements of 13-35%)

• Reduces anxiety before high-pressure situations

• Accelerates skill acquisition when combined with physical practice

• Increases motivation and goal-directed behavior

• Enhances creative problem-solving abilities

Types of Visualization for Achievement

Process Visualization Mentally rehearsing the specific steps and actions required to achieve your goal. This type of visualization focuses on the journey rather than just the destination. **When to use**: Before learning new skills, when preparing for challenging tasks, or when developing new habits **When to use:** Before learning new skills, when preparing for challenging tasks, or when developing new habits **Identity Visualization** Imagining yourself as the person who has already developed the qualities, habits, and skills you're working to build. This helps bridge the gap between your current and ideal self. **When to use:** When working on character development, during major life transitions, or when breaking limiting beliefs	Outcome Visualization Creating vivid mental images of successfully achieving your desired result. This generates positive emotions and strengthens belief in your ability to succeed. **When to use:** When setting new goals, during moments of doubt, or as motivation during challenging periods **Problem-Solving Visualization** Mentally exploring different approaches to a challenge, allowing your mind to generate creative solutions that logical thinking alone might miss. **When to use:** When facing complex problems, during creative blocks, or when standard approaches aren't working **When to use:** When facing complex problems, during creative blocks, or when standard approaches aren't working

Exercise: The PESI Visualization Method

For maximum effectiveness, use the PESI method to structure your visualization practice:

1. P - Prepare: Find a quiet place, close your eyes, and take several deep breaths to enter a relaxed state

2. E - Engage: Fully engage all your senses in the visualization (what you see, hear, feel, smell, and taste)

3. S - Specific: Include specific details rather than vague images

4. I - Internal: Focus on internal feelings of competence and confidence as much as external circumstances

Practice for 5-10 minutes daily, ideally just before performing the visualized activity or immediately after journaling about your goals.

Advanced Visualization Techniques

Mental Contrasting Alternate between visualizing your desired outcome and potential obstacles you might face. This approach, backed by research from psychologist Gabriele Oettingen, helps generate realistic strategies for overcoming challenges. **How to practice**: Visualize your goal in detail for 3-5 minutes, then spend 3-5 minutes imagining obstacles and how you'll overcome them Multiple Scenario Visualization Visualize multiple possible scenarios for a particular situation, preparing your mind to be flexible and adaptive. This technique is	Timeline Visualization Create a mental timeline from your current position to your future goal, visualizing key milestones along the way. This helps break down large goals into manageable steps and creates a sense of progress. **How to practice**: Imagine a road or path leading to your goal, with clear markers representing important progress points Third-Person Perspective Sometimes viewing yourself from an outside perspective (as if watching a movie of yourself) provides greater insights and emotional regulation than first-person visualization.

especially useful for situations with uncertain outcomes. **How to practice:** For any important upcoming event, visualize three different scenarios: best case, worst case, and most likely case	**How to practice**: Alternate between first-person ("through your own eyes") and third-person ("watching yourself") perspectives during visualization

From Visualization to Reality: Dr. Maxwell Maltz's Research

Dr. Maxwell Maltz, a plastic surgeon who wrote the influential book "Psycho-Cybernetics," observed that it takes about 21 days for patients to adjust to their new appearance after surgery. This led him to research how mental imagery affects physical outcomes.

In one famous experiment, three groups of basketball players were tested on free throw shooting:

• Group 1 practiced free throws physically for 20 minutes daily

• Group 2 only visualized shooting free throws for 20 minutes daily

• Group 3 did a combination: 10 minutes of physical practice and 10 minutes of visualization

After 30 days, Group 1 improved by 24%, Group 2 improved by 23% (nearly the same as physical practice!), and Group 3 improved by 32%—showing that the combination of physical practice and visualization produces the best results.

This research demonstrates that visualization is not just positive thinking—it's a form of mental training that creates measurable changes in performance.

Self-Talk: Programming Your Internal Dialogue

The conversations you have with yourself shape your reality more than any external voice. Self-talk—your internal dialogue—determines your emotional state, your decisions, and ultimately your results.

Psychologists estimate that we speak to ourselves at a rate of 150-300 words per minute, adding up to approximately 50,000 thoughts per day. The quality and pattern of this internal dialogue dramatically affects everything from your confidence and resilience to your problem-solving abilities and relationships.

The Impact of Negative vs. Positive Self-Talk

Negative Self-Talk Patterns	Impact on Performance
"I'm not good enough for this"	Reduces effort, increases anxiety, creates self-fulfilling prophecy of failure
"I always mess things up"	Creates defeatist mindset, blinds you to learning opportunities
"This is too hard/complicated"	Decreases persistence, prevents development of problem-solving strategies
"What will others think if I fail?"	Increases performance anxiety, leads to avoidance of challenges

Positive Self-Talk Patterns	Impact on Performance
"I'm prepared and capable"	Increases confidence, reduces performance anxiety
"I learn and grow from every experience"	Creates growth mindset, enhances learning from setbacks
"I can figure this out step by step"	Improves problem-solving, increases persistence
"I focus on my own progress, not others' opinions"	Develops internal validation, reduces social anxiety

Transforming Your Self-Talk

Changing your internal dialogue isn't about forced positivity—it's about developing more accurate, helpful, and constructive patterns of thinking. Here's a systematic approach to transforming your self-talk:

1. Awareness: Begin by simply noticing your current self-talk patterns. What do you say to yourself when facing challenges? When making mistakes? When considering new opportunities?

2. Identification: Identify specific negative patterns using the common categories below

3. Challenge: Question the accuracy and helpfulness of negative self-talk

4. Replace: Develop alternative statements that are both realistic and supportive

5. Practice: Consistently use the new statements, especially during challenging situations

All-or-Nothing Thinking	Overgeneralization
Negative pattern: "If I don't do this perfectly, I'm a complete failure." **Empowering alternative:** "I don't need to be perfect to make progress. Every step forward counts." **Mental Filtering Negative pattern:** "They gave me one piece of criticism, so my entire project must be terrible." **Empowering alternative:** "There were many positive aspects to my work, and this feedback helps me improve specific areas." Jumping to Conclusions **Negative pattern:** "They didn't respond to my email. They must be upset with me." **Empowering alternative:** "There could be many reasons for the delay that have nothing to do with me. I'll follow up appropriately."	**Negative pattern:** "I messed up this presentation. I always fail at public speaking." **Empowering alternative:** "This presentation didn't go as planned, but I've had successful ones before and can learn from this experience." **Empowering alternative:** "There were many positive aspects to my work, and this feedback helps me improve specific areas." **Disqualifying the Positive Negative pattern:** "I only succeeded because I got lucky" or "Anyone could have done that." **Empowering alternative:** "My preparation and skills contributed significantly to this success." **Catastrophizing Negative pattern:** "If I make a mistake in this presentation, my career will be over." **Empowering alternative:** "Even if I make a mistake, it will be a learning experience, not a catastrophe."

Self-Talk Transformation Worksheet

Step 1: Record your negative self-talk statements for one week. Notice when and where they occur most frequently.

____

____

Step 2: Identify the pattern each statement falls into (all-or-nothing, overgeneralization, etc.).

____

____

Step 3: Create empowering alternatives for your most common negative statements.

Negative Statement	Pattern	Empowering Alternative

The Power of Affirmations and Incantations

Affirmations are positive statements that, when repeated regularly, help reprogram your subconscious mind. While sometimes dismissed as simplistic, research in neuroscience confirms that consistent repetition of specific phrases can create new neural pathways and belief patterns.

For maximum effectiveness, follow these guidelines when creating affirmations:

1. Present tense: Frame affirmations as if they're already true ("I am" not "I will be")

2. Positive language: State what you want, not what you don't want

3. Personal: Begin with "I" or your name

4. Specific: Target precise outcomes or qualities

5. Emotional: Include feeling words that create an emotional response

6. Realistic: Choose statements that stretch but don't strain belief

Incantations: Affirmations with Power

Tony Robbins differentiates between affirmations (statements repeated mentally) and incantations (statements spoken aloud with physical and emotional intensity). The addition of physical movement and emotional energy dramatically increases the impact on your nervous system.

To practice incantations:

1. Stand in a power position (upright, shoulders back, head high)

2. Speak your statements aloud with conviction and energy

3. Add physical movement (gestures, facial expressions, whole-body movement)

4. Infuse each statement with genuine emotion

Example: While punching the air with energy, declaring loudly and confidently: "I am unstoppable! I turn challenges into opportunities! Every day I grow stronger and more capable!"

Integration: Creating Your Mind Programming Routine

The true power of these practices emerges when they're combined into a consistent routine. Here's a suggested 15-minute daily mind programming session that integrates journaling, visualization, and self-talk:

1. Journaling (5 minutes): Record three gratitudes, your primary focus for the day, and one challenge you're currently facing

2. Empowering Self-Talk (3 minutes): Write and then say aloud 3-5 affirmations related to your current goals and challenges

3. Visualization (5 minutes): Visualize yourself successfully navigating your day and making progress on your most important goal

4. Physical Anchoring (2 minutes): Create a physical gesture (like pressing your thumb and forefinger together) while in a peak state, then use this gesture throughout the day to quickly recall positive emotions and focus

Consistency is more important than duration. A daily 15-minute practice will create far greater results than an occasional hour-long session.

In the next chapter, we'll explore how to track your progress and build accountability systems that ensure consistent growth and development.

6.3 Tracking Progress & Building Accountability

What gets measured gets improved. While the previous chapters have equipped you with powerful daily practices, this chapter focuses on how to monitor your progress and create accountability systems that ensure consistent advancement toward your goals.

Without proper tracking and accountability, even the most motivated individuals can drift off course. Our minds are naturally biased toward overestimating our progress and underestimating our setbacks. Objective tracking systems counteract these biases, providing an accurate picture of where you stand and what needs adjustment.

The Psychology of Tracking and Measurement

Tracking your progress isn't just about data collection—it fundamentally changes your behavior through several psychological mechanisms:

1. **The Hawthorne Effect:** The simple act of measuring a behavior tends to improve that behavior. When you know you're tracking something, your awareness and intention around that area naturally increase.

2. **Feedback Loops:** Tracking creates immediate feedback that allows for rapid course correction. Without this feedback, small deviations can become major derailments before you notice.

3. **Progress Principle:** Research by Harvard's Teresa Amabile shows that visible progress is the single most powerful motivator in complex work. Tracking systems make progress visible, even when it might otherwise feel imperceptible.

4. **Consistency Principle:** We have a psychological drive to remain consistent with our prior actions and commitments. Tracking creates a record that leverages this drive, making it more likely you'll follow through.

What to Track: The Key Success Metrics

Effective tracking focuses on both leading and lagging indicators across each life pillar:

• **Leading indicators** are the daily actions and habits that predict future results (e.g., workouts completed, meditation sessions, networking conversations)

• **Lagging indicators** are the results that come from those actions (e.g., weight, energy levels, income, relationship satisfaction)

Here are the most important metrics to track in each life pillar:

Health Metrics Leading:	Wealth Metrics Leading:	Relationships Metrics Leading:
Exercise sessions (frequency, duration, intensity) Sleep quality and duration Water intake Nutritional choices Meditation/stress management practice	Income-generating activities Learning/skill development time Networking/relationship building Applications/outreach activities Ideas generated and tested	Quality time with key people Meaningful conversations Acts of appreciation/service New connections made Conflict resolution attempts
Lagging: Weight/body composition Energy levels Resting heart rate Mood and mental clarity Health markers (BP, cholesterol, etc.)	**Lagging:** Income from all sources Savings rate Net worth Debt reduction Investment growth Personal Growth Metrics **Leading:**	**Lagging:** Relationship satisfaction Support network strength Sense of belonging/connection Trust levels in key relationships

Purpose/Career Metrics	Journal entries completed	Communication effectiveness
Leading: Time spent on meaningful work Learning activities in your field Skills practice sessions Value-aligned actions Creative output	Books read / courses taken Meditation/reflection time Comfort zone challenges Feedback actively sought	Happiness/Fulfillment Metrics **Leading:** Gratitude practice Flow state experiences Present-moment awareness Time spent on enjoyable activities Celebration of wins
Lagging: Career advancement Skill mastery levels Work satisfaction Impact on others Recognition in your field	**Lagging:** Self-awareness level Emotional regulation ability Growth mindset strength Resilience in challenges Wisdom applied to decisions	**Lagging:** Overall life satisfaction Sense of meaning and purpose Positive to negative emotion ratio Engagement in daily activities Optimism about the future

The Rule of 3-5 Metrics

While the lists above are comprehensive, trying to track everything leads to overwhelm and abandonment. For sustainable tracking, focus on just 3-5 metrics in each life area that are:

1. High-leverage: Strongly correlated with your desired outcomes

2. Actionable: Within your control to change

3. Easy to measure: Simple enough to track consistently

For example, in health, you might track: daily steps, hours of sleep, water intake, and weekly workout sessions—all simple to measure yet highly impactful.

Tracking Systems: From Simple to Sophisticated

The best tracking system is the one you'll actually use consistently. Here are options ranging from low-tech to digital:

<table>
<tr>
<td>

1. Habit Tracker in Journal
A simple grid with habits listed vertically and dates horizontally, with boxes to check or fill when complete. This visual approach is highly effective for building consistency.

Best for: Daily habits, simple metrics, visual motivation

</td>
<td>

2. Bullet Journal Method
A highly flexible system using a notebook with various modules for tracking habits, projects, goals, and reflections—all indexed for easy reference.

Best for: Creative types, those who enjoy customization, comprehensive life tracking

</td>
</tr>
<tr>
<td>

3. Digital Habit Apps
Applications like Habitica, Streaks, or Habit Bull that gamify tracking and provide notifications, statistics, and visual progress indicators.

Best for: Tech-savvy individuals, those motivated by gamification, detailed analytics

</td>
<td>

4. Specialized Tracking Apps
Domain-specific applications like fitness trackers (Strava, MyFitnessPal), finance apps (Mint, YNAB), or productivity trackers (RescueTime, Toggl).

Best for: Deep tracking in specific life areas, automatic data collection

</td>
</tr>
<tr>
<td>

5. Spreadsheet Systems
Custom Excel or Google Sheets that can be tailored to track exactly what matters to you, with options for graphs, calculations, and data analysis.

Best for: Analytical types, those who want custom calculations, comprehensive data views

</td>
<td>

6. Journal + Photo Documentation
Combining written tracking with visual documentation through photos creates a powerful record of change over time.

Best for: Visual learners, physical transformations, creative projects

</td>
</tr>
</table>

Exercise: Creating Your Personal Dashboard

A personal dashboard brings together your most important metrics in one place for easy daily review. Follow these steps to create yours:

1. Select 1-2 leading indicators and 1 lagging indicator from each life pillar (no more than 15 total metrics)

2. Determine the ideal tracking frequency for each (daily, weekly, monthly)

3. Choose a simple system to record these metrics (paper or digital)

4. Design a weekly review process to assess patterns and make adjustments

Example: A basic dashboard might track daily meditation (minutes), exercise (yes/no), reading (pages), income-generating activities (number), meaningful conversations (number), and weekly ratings (1-10) of energy, finances, relationship quality, and work satisfaction.

The Power of Regular Reviews

Data collection without reflection is merely record-keeping. The true power of tracking emerges when you regularly review your data to extract insights and make adjustments. Establish a rhythm of reviews at different intervals:

Daily Review (5 minutes)	Weekly Review (20-30 minutes)	Monthly Review (60 minutes)
Record today's metrics	Analyze patterns across metrics	Evaluate progress toward larger goals
Acknowledge wins, however small	Calculate weekly averages/totals	Identify what's working and what isn't
Note any patterns or challenges	Compare to previous weeks	Adjust targets if needed
Set intentions for tomorrow	Adjust plans for the coming week	Set focus areas for the coming month
	Celebrate progress and wins	Acknowledge and celebrate growth

The Review Ritual

Make your reviews more effective by creating a ritual around them:

- Schedule them at the same time each day/week/month

- Create a pleasant environment (favorite café, comfortable home space)

- Begin with a few minutes of mindfulness to clear your mind

- Use specific reflection questions to guide your thinking

- End by capturing key insights and specific next actions

Building Accountability Systems

While tracking provides awareness, accountability creates the external pressure that often makes the difference between intention and action. Effective accountability combines consequences, commitments to others, and environmental design.

Types of Accountability Systems

1. Accountability Partners A dedicated person who checks in on your progress regularly and holds you to your commitments. This could be a friend, colleague, or family member with similar goals. **How to implement**: Set up weekly check-ins where you each share progress on your goals, challenges faced, and plans for the coming week. Be specific about what you want them to hold you accountable for. 3. Coaches and Mentors Professional guidance from someone with expertise in your area of focus, combining	2. Mastermind Groups A small group (typically 4-8 people) that meets regularly to support each member's goals through shared learning, accountability, and problem-solving. How to implement: Form a group that meets bi-weekly or monthly, with each person sharing updates, getting feedback, and committing to specific actions before the next meeting. 4. Public Declarations Leveraging social pressure by publicly stating your goals and regularly updating your community on your progress.

accountability with strategic direction and feedback.

How to implement: Invest in regular sessions with a coach in your field, setting clear goals and reporting on progress between meetings.

5. Financial Stakes
Creating meaningful financial consequences for following through (or not) on your commitments.

How to implement: Use services like StickK or Beeminder that let you put money on the line, or make a bet with a friend where you forfeit money if you don't follow through.

How to implement: Share your goals on social media, with your team, or with your family, then provide consistent updates on your journey.

6. Progress Visualization
Making your progress (or lack thereof) highly visible to create constant environmental triggers.

How to implement: Use visual trackers displayed prominently in your environment—progress bars, charts on the wall, or physical representations of achievements.

Creating an Effective Accountability Partnership

Among accountability systems, partnerships are often the most accessible and effective. Here's how to create one that drives real results:

1. **Choose the right partner**: Look for someone who is:

- Committed to their own goals (not just helping you)
- Reliable and consistent
- Comfortable with honesty and direct communication
- Supportive but not enabling

2. **Set clear expectations:**

- Meeting frequency and format (in-person, video, text)
- Preparation required before each check-in
- Communication between formal check-ins
- How to handle missed commitments

3. **Structure your check-ins: Use a consistent format, such as:**

- Wins and progress since last check-in (5 minutes each)
- Challenges and obstacles faced (5 minutes each)
- Specific commitments for the coming period (5 minutes each)
- Support needed from partner (5 minutes each)

4. **Create meaningful consequences:**

- Accountability works best when there are real stakes
- Agree on consequences for missed commitments
- These can be financial, social, or related to extra work

5. **Review and adjust the partnership:**

- Every 1-2 months, evaluate how the partnership is working
- Adjust frequency, format, or focus areas as needed
- Acknowledge the impact you're having on each other's progress

Accountability Partnership Agreement

Our Goals: We commit to supporting each other in achieving the following goals:

Partner 1 (Your Name): ________________________________

Partner 2 (Partner's Name): ________________________________

Check-in Schedule:

☐ Weekly (Day/Time): ________________

☐ Bi-weekly (Day/Time): ________________

☐ Monthly (Day/Time): ________________

☐ Other: ________________

Check-in Format:

☐ In-person

☐ Video call

☐ Phone call

☐ Text/email

Consequences for Missed Commitments:

____

Additional Agreements:

____

Signatures:

____

____

Date: ____________________

Overcoming Common Tracking and Accountability Challenges

Challenge: Inconsistent Tracking **Solutions:**	Challenge: Data Without Insight **Solutions:**
Simplify your system to track fewer metrics Use habit stacking (attach tracking to an existing habit)	Schedule regular review sessions with specific reflection questions Look for correlations between different metrics

Set up reminders or triggers in your environment Create a "minimum viable tracking" version for busy days Challenge: Accountability Fatigue **Solutions:** Rotate accountability methods to maintain freshness Balance accountability with celebration of wins Build in "rest periods" where accountability is lighter Ensure your accountability system includes support, not just checking	Share your data with someone who can provide an outside perspective Focus on identifying patterns rather than individual data points Challenge: Shame Spirals After Missed Targets Solutions: Focus on learning rather than judgment when reviewing data Use "never miss twice" rule—one miss is a data point, two is a pattern Analyze obstacles objectively: what specifically prevented success? Design your next action to be small enough to ensure a win

From Struggling to Thriving: Maria's Accountability System

Maria had been trying to build her freelance business for years while working full-time, but repeatedly found herself procrastinating on essential business-building activities. Despite having clear goals and knowing what she needed to do, weeks would pass with minimal progress.

She implemented a multi-layered accountability system:

1. Daily tracking: She created a simple spreadsheet to track two key metrics—hours spent on her business and number of potential client outreaches

2. Weekly accountability partner: She partnered with another freelancer for Sunday evening check-ins where they reviewed progress and set next week's commitments

3. Monthly mastermind: She joined a group of six entrepreneurs who met monthly for deeper strategy discussions and long-term accountability

4. Quarterly coach: She invested in quarterly sessions with a business coach who helped her set strategic directions and evaluate progress

5. Public declaration: She started a newsletter where she shared her business journey with subscribers, creating social accountability

Within six months, this layered approach led to consistent action, doubled her client base, and allowed her to reduce her full-time hours to part-time. The key wasn't just the individual systems but how they complemented each other—daily tracking for awareness, weekly check-ins for consistent action, monthly mastermind for strategy, quarterly coaching for course **correction, and public sharing for motivation.**

Bringing It All Together: Your Progress and Accountability Plan

Now it's time to design your personal tracking and accountability system. Remember that the best system is one you'll actually use consistently, so start simple and build as habits form.

Progress and Accountability Plan

Step 1: Select your key metrics (3-5 per life pillar)

Health:

____

Wealth:

____

Relationships:

____

Purpose/Career:

____

Step 2: Choose your tracking system

☐   Paper journal/habit tracker

☐   Digital app (specify): _____________________

☐   Spreadsheet

☐   Combination (describe): _____________________

Step 3: Set your review schedule

Daily review time: _____________________

Weekly review day/time: _____________________

Monthly review day/time: _____________________

Step 4: Select your accountability approaches (choose at least two)

☐   Accountability partner (who: _____________________)

☐   Mastermind group

☐   Coach/mentor

☐   Public declaration

☐   Financial stakes

☐   Progress visualization

☐   Other: _____________________

Step 5: Implementation plan

When will you start this system? _____________________

What preparations are needed before starting? _____________________

Potential obstacles and how you'll overcome them:

As you implement your tracking and accountability system, remember that the purpose is progress, not perfection. Use these tools to gain insights and motivation, not as another source of stress or self-judgment.

In the next chapter, we'll bring everything together with a comprehensive 90-Day Freedom Plan that will help you transform your life using all the strategies we've covered so far.

6.4 90-Day Freedom Plan

Now it's time to integrate everything you've learned into a comprehensive 90-day plan that will transform your life. Why 90 days? Research shows this timeframe is ideal for meaningful change—long enough to see significant results but short enough to maintain focus and motivation.

A 90-day horizon strikes the perfect balance between short-term action and long-term vision. It provides enough time to build new habits, see measurable progress, and make course corrections, yet it's not so distant that your goals feel abstract or your motivation wanes.

The Science of Rapid Transformation

90-day transformation periods work because they align with several principles of behavioral science:

1. Parkinson's Law: "Work expands to fill the time available for its completion." A defined 90-day window creates healthy time pressure that increases focus and prevents procrastination.

2. Neuroplasticity Timeline: Research suggests that new neural pathways begin to solidify after about 30 days of consistent practice, and become more automatic by 60-90 days.

3. Motivation Cycle: Most people experience natural motivation cycles, with initial enthusiasm, a middle period of challenge, and renewed energy as visible results appear. A 90-day framework accommodates this full cycle.

4. Compound Effect: Small, consistent actions compound dramatically over 90 days, often creating breakthrough results just as motivation might otherwise wane.

The Four Phases of Your 90-Day Freedom Plan

Your 90-day journey will unfold in four distinct phases, each with its own focus and objectives:

<table>
<tr><td>

Phase 1: Foundation (Days 1-15)
The first two weeks are about establishing baselines, setting clear goals, and creating the systems that will support your journey.

Key activities:
• Complete assessments in each life pillar
• Set specific 90-day goals and milestones
• Establish morning and evening routines
• Set up tracking and accountability systems
• Prepare your environment for success

Phase 3: Acceleration (Days 46-75)
As habits become more automatic, this phase focuses on deepening practice and accelerating results.

Key activities:
• Increasing intensity or duration of practices
• Leveraging early results for greater momentum
• Adding complementary habits or skills

</td><td>

Phase 2: Momentum (Days 16-45)
The next month focuses on building consistent habits and generating early wins that create momentum.

Key activities:
• Daily practice of core habits
• Weekly review and adjustment
• Regular accountability
• check-ins
• Overcoming initial obstacles
• Celebrating small wins

Phase 4: Integration (Days 76-90)
The final phase solidifies your progress and prepares for sustainable long-term growth.

Key activities:
• Ensuring habits are fully integrated into lifestyle
• Comprehensive progress assessment
• Celebration of achievements
• Planning for the next 90-day cycle

</td></tr>
</table>

• Mid-point assessment and course correction • Addressing more challenging obstacles	•Adjusting systems for long-term sustainability

Creating Your Personalized 90-Day Plan

While the framework above provides structure, your 90-day plan needs to be personalized to your specific goals and circumstances. Let's walk through the process of creating your plan step by step.

Step 1: Assess Your Current Reality

Begin by taking honest stock of where you stand in each life pillar. Rate your current satisfaction on a scale of 1-10 and identify specific strengths and challenges.

Current Reality Assessment

Life Pillar	Current Rating (1-10)	Current Strengths	Current Challenges
Health			
Wealth			
Relationships			
Purpose/Career			

Step 2: Set Compelling 90-Day Goals

For each life pillar, set one primary goal that would significantly improve your life if achieved within 90 days. Ensure your goals follow the SMART+ criteria:

- Specific: Clearly defined with no ambiguity

- Measurable: Includes concrete metrics to track progress

- Achievable: Challenging but realistic within 90 days

- Relevant: Aligned with your deeper values and long-term vision

- Time-bound: Has specific deadlines (final and milestones)

- +Emotionally Engaging: Genuinely excites and motivates you

90-Day SMART+ Goals

Health Goal:

____

Why this matters to me:

____

How I'll measure success:

____

Wealth Goal:

____

Why this matters to me:

____

____

How I'll measure success:

____

Relationships Goal:

____

Why this matters to me:

____

How I'll measure success:

____

Purpose/Career Goal:

____

Why this matters to me:

____

How I'll measure success:

____

Step 3: Break Down Goals Into Milestones

Divide each 90-day goal into three 30-day milestones. This creates a clear path of progression and allows for regular celebration of wins.

Goal	30-Day Milestone	60-Day Milestone	90-Day Milestone
Health Goal			
Wealth Goal			
Relationships Goal			
Purpose/Career Goal			

Step 4: Identify Key Habits and Actions

For each goal, determine the daily and weekly habits or actions that will drive progress. These become your leading indicators to track.

Key Habits and Actions

Health Goal:

Daily habits:

____

Weekly actions:

____

Wealth Goal:

Daily habits:

____

Weekly actions:

____

Relationships Goal:

Daily habits:

____

Weekly actions:

____

Purpose/Career Goal:

Daily habits:

____

Weekly actions:

____

Step 5: Design Your Support Systems

Identify the systems, tools, and people that will support your success.

Support Systems

Daily Routines: (Morning/evening routines that will support your goals)

____

Tracking Systems: (How you'll monitor progress on your habits and goals)

____

Accountability: (People or systems that will hold you accountable)

____

Environment Design: (Changes to your physical environment to support success)

____

Resources Needed: (Books, tools, services, or other resources)

____

Step 6: Anticipate and Plan for Obstacles

Identify potential challenges and create specific strategies to overcome them.

Obstacle Planning

Potential Obstacle	Prevention Strategy	Contingency Plan

Step 7: Create Your Weekly Implementation Plan

Break down your first 30 days into specific weekly plans. You'll update this plan at the end of each week for the coming week.

Week 1 Implementation Plan

Focus for the week:

____

Daily non-negotiable habits:

____

Key actions to complete this week:

____

Specific scheduling: (When exactly will you complete each action?)

____

Support and accountability for this week:

Phase-Specific Strategies for Maximum Results

Each phase of your 90-day journey requires different approaches to maximize progress. Here are specific strategies for each phase:

Phase 1: Foundation (Days 1-15) Strategies

1. Start small to build confidence: Begin with habits that take 5 minutes or less to build early momentum and confidence

2. Create environmental triggers: Set up physical reminders and cues in your environment that prompt your new habits

3. Eliminate friction: Remove obstacles to your key habits (e.g., laying out workout clothes the night before, preparing healthy meals in advance)

4. Focus on consistency over intensity: It's better to meditate for 5 minutes daily than 35 minutes once a week

5. Overcommit to accountability: In this early phase, use multiple accountability methods to ensure you establish momentum

The 2-Minute Rule for Habit Formation

When starting a new habit, make the initial version so easy it takes less than 2 minutes to complete. This removes resistance and establishes the behavioral pattern:

- "Read for an hour" becomes "Read one page"

- "Write a chapter" becomes "Write one sentence"

- "Run 5K" becomes "Put on running shoes and step outside"

Once the 2-minute version becomes a consistent habit, you can gradually increase the duration or intensity.

Phase 2: Momentum (Days 16-45) Strategies

1. Gradually increase challenge: As foundational habits become consistent, slowly increase duration, intensity, or complexity

2. Implement habit stacking: Attach new habits to established ones (e.g., "After I brush my teeth, I will meditate for 10 minutes")

3. Create streak tracking: Maintain visual records of your consistency to leverage the psychological power of "not breaking the chain"

4. Develop failure recovery protocols: Create specific plans for how you'll get back on track immediately after missing a habit

5. Begin journaling on progress: Regularly write about your experiences, challenges, and insights to deepen your commitment

Momentum Phase Success: James's Story

James struggled with consistency in his health goals for years. In his 90-day plan, he used these momentum-building strategies:

• Started with a 10-minute morning walk, gradually increasing to 30 minutes by day 45

• Used habit stacking by drinking a glass of water every time he checked his phone (linking a new habit to an existing trigger)

• Created a wall calendar where he marked each day he completed his habits, building an unbroken chain

• Developed a "never miss twice" rule—if he missed a day, he committed to a minimal version the next day no matter what

• Journaled for 5 minutes every evening about his health choices and how they aligned with his values

By day 45, James had lost 12 pounds, established consistent exercise and nutrition habits, and most importantly, had broken his pattern of starting and stopping health initiatives.

Phase 3: Acceleration (Days 46-75) Strategies

1. Conduct a mid-point review: Assess progress on all goals, celebrating wins and adjusting strategies as needed

2. Look for leverage points: Identify specific actions that are producing the most results and double down on them

3. Address secondary obstacles: Now that fundamental habits are established, tackle more complex challenges

4. Increase accountability intensity: Raise the stakes on your accountability systems to push through the middle-phase plateau

5. Seek expert feedback: Consult with mentors or experts who can help refine your approach for greater results

The 80/20 Principle in Goal Achievement

During your acceleration phase, apply the Pareto Principle (80% of results come from 20% of efforts) by asking:

1. Which 20% of my daily/weekly actions are producing 80% of my results?

2. Which 20% of my obstacles are causing 80% of my setbacks?

3. Which 20% of my relationships are providing 80% of my support?

By identifying these high-leverage areas, you can focus your energy where it will create the greatest acceleration of results.

Phase 4: Integration (Days 76-90) Strategies

1. Focus on habit automation: Work on making key habits more automatic and less dependent on willpower or external accountability

2. Conduct environment optimization: Make final adjustments to your physical and social environment to support long-term success

3. Create maintenance protocols: Develop systems for maintaining your progress during challenging periods (travel, illness, high stress)

4. Design celebration rituals: Plan meaningful ways to acknowledge and celebrate your achievements

5. Prepare your next 90-day plan: Use insights from this cycle to design an even more effective next phase

Integration Phase Planning

Habits to automate: (Which key habits need to become more automatic?)

Environment adjustments: (What final changes will support long-term success?)

Maintenance protocols: (How will you maintain progress during challenging periods?)

Celebration plan: (How will you meaningfully celebrate your achievements?)

Next cycle focus areas: (Based on this cycle, what should you focus on next?)

The Weekly Review and Planning Ritual

The most critical component of your 90-day plan is the weekly review and planning session. This 60-minute ritual keeps you on track, allows for necessary adjustments, and maintains your focus and motivation.

Schedule this session at the same time each week (many find Sunday evening or Monday morning most effective) and follow this structured process:

Weekly Review and Planning Process

Part 1: Review the Past Week (25 minutes)

1. Review your tracking data (5 minutes)

- What habits and actions did you complete consistently?

- Where did you miss or struggle?

- What patterns do you notice?

2. **Celebrate wins and progress (5 minutes)**

- What specific achievements are you proud of?

- What progress did you make toward your 90-day goals?

- What did you learn or what skills did you develop?

3. **Analyze challenges (10 minutes)**

- What specific obstacles or setbacks did you face?

- What was the root cause of each challenge?

- What adjustments could prevent or better address these challenges?

4. **Extract lessons and insights (5 minutes)**

- What did you learn about yourself this week?

- What strategies proved most effective?

- What would you do differently next time?

Part 2: Plan the Coming Week (35 minutes)

5. Review your 90-day goals and current phase (5 minutes)

- Reconnect with your 90-day goals and why they matter

- Consider which phase you're in and the appropriate strategies

- Check your 30-day milestone progress

6. Set your weekly focus and intentions (5 minutes)

- What is your primary focus for the coming week?

- What specific outcome would make this week successful?

- What mindset or approach do you want to bring to the week?

7. Plan your key actions and habits (15 minutes)

- What daily habits will you commit to?

- What specific actions will move you toward your milestones?

- When exactly will you complete these actions? (Schedule them)

8. Prepare for obstacles (5 minutes)

- What challenges might arise this week?

- What specific strategies will you use to overcome them?

- What contingency plans should you have ready?

9. Set up accountability and support (5 minutes)

- Who needs to know about your plans?

- What accountability check-ins will you arrange?

- What support might you need, and how will you ask for it?

Staying Motivated Throughout Your 90-Day Journey

Even with the best planning, motivation will naturally fluctuate throughout your 90-day journey. Here are strategies to maintain momentum during challenging periods:

<table>
<tr><td>

1. Connect With Your Why
Regularly revisit the deeper reasons behind your goals. Create a "why statement" that emotionally resonates with you, and read it daily. Consider creating a vision board that visually represents what you're working toward.

3. Create Celebration Rituals
Plan meaningful rewards for reaching milestones. These should align with your goals (not undermine them) and provide genuine satisfaction. The anticipation of earned rewards can pull you through difficult periods.

5. Use Identity-Based Motivation
Focus on the person you're becoming rather than just the goals you're achieving. Ask "What would a healthy person do?" rather than "Should I exercise today?" This identity-based approach is more sustainable than outcome-based motivation.

</td><td>

2. Use Progress Visibility
Make your progress highly visible. Use visual trackers, progress photos, or milestone markers to see how far you've come. The visual evidence of progress is a powerful motivator when willpower wanes.

4. Leverage Social Commitment
Increase your public commitment during motivational dips. Share your journey with others, join communities with similar goals, or use social media as an accountability platform. Social commitment often provides motivation when personal willpower is low.

6. Create Motivation Emergency Kits
Prepare for motivation dips by creating resources you can turn to: inspirational videos or articles, supportive messages from friends, reminders of past successes, or powerful quotes. Have these ready for when you need them most.

</td></tr>
</table>

The Complete 90-Day Transformation: Priya's Story

Priya, a 34-year-old marketing manager, felt stuck in every area of her life. She was 25 pounds overweight, constantly stressed, in debt, and feeling disconnected from her purpose.

She implemented a comprehensive 90-day plan focusing on all four life pillars:

• Health goal: Lose 15 pounds and establish a sustainable exercise routine

• Wealth goal: Create a budget, reduce expenses by 20%, and start a $1000 emergency fund

• Relationships goal: Rebuild connection with three key people and establish weekly quality time

• Purpose goal: Clarify career direction and develop one marketable skill aligned with her interests

Her key implementation strategies included:

• Morning routine: 20 minutes of meditation, journaling, and planning

• Daily habit tracking using a simple app

• Weekly reviews every Sunday evening

• Accountability partner with bi-weekly video calls

• Environment redesign: removed tempting foods, created a meditation space, automated savings

By the end of 90 days, Priya had lost 18 pounds, built a $1200 emergency fund, repaired important relationships, and discovered a passion for content strategy that led to new career opportunities. More important than these external results was her increased sense of control, confidence, and clarity about her future.

From 90 Days to a Lifetime of Freedom

Your 90-day plan is not just about achieving specific goals—it's about establishing the foundation for a lifetime of growth and freedom. As you approach the end of your 90 days, consider these strategies for sustaining your momentum:

1. Conduct a comprehensive review: Thoroughly assess what worked, what didn't, and what you learned about yourself during the process

2. Establish maintenance systems: Create simplified versions of your tracking and accountability systems that can be sustained long-term

3. Design your next 90-day cycle: Building on your current success, set new goals that continue your growth trajectory

4. Focus on habit depth: Rather than constantly adding new habits, work on deepening and improving your existing key habits

5. Share your journey: Consider mentoring or supporting others on similar journeys, which reinforces your own progress

The Compound Effect of Consecutive 90-Day Cycles

The true power of the 90-day approach emerges when you complete multiple consecutive cycles. Each cycle builds on the previous one, creating compound growth:

First 90 days: Establish foundation and basic habits

7. Real Stories of Freedom & Transformation

Throughout this book, we've explored strategies and frameworks for breaking free from stagnation and creating a life of purpose, freedom, and fulfillment. But concepts alone aren't enough—it's in the application and real-world results where true transformation happens.

In this final part, we'll explore real stories of people who have applied the principles we've discussed to transform their lives. These aren't overnight success stories with unrealistic outcomes. They're honest accounts of real struggle, persistence, and eventual breakthrough. Each story demonstrates how ordinary people have achieved extraordinary results by implementing the systems and mindsets we've covered throughout this book.

As you read these stories, look for yourself in them. See how the challenges these individuals faced might mirror your own. More importantly, recognize that if they could overcome their obstacles, so can you. Their stories aren't meant to be simply inspirational—they're meant to be instructional, showing you the path forward through real-world examples.

Let's begin with people who turned their lives around when they felt stuck, just as you might feel now.

7.1 Case Studies: People Who Turned Their Life Around

Raj's Story: From Burnout to Balance

Health Wealth Relationships Purpose

At 32, Raj had what many would consider a successful life on paper. A senior software engineer at a prestigious tech company, he had a six-figure salary, a beautiful apartment in Bangalore, and the respect of his peers. But beneath the surface, his life was crumbling.

"I was working 70-hour weeks, surviving on coffee and takeout, and hadn't seen my parents in over eight months despite living in the same city," Raj recalls. "My relationships were superficial, my health was deteriorating with rapid weight gain and constant fatigue, and despite my 'success,' I felt empty and directionless."

The breaking point came after a panic attack during an important client meeting. Forced to take a medical leave, Raj was confronted with the reality that his life had become unbalanced to the point of physical collapse.

Turning Point Moment:

"During my medical leave, I was scrolling through photos on my phone and realized I hadn't taken a single picture in the past year that wasn't work-related. No family gatherings, no personal achievements, no moments of joy. That's when it hit me—I wasn't really living; I was just existing for my job."

Raj began rebuilding his life by applying the Four Life Pillars Audit (as described in Chapter 1.4). The results were eye-opening: his health and relationships scored below 3 out of 10, while his wealth was high but his sense of purpose was completely missing.

Steps Raj Took to Transform His Life:

1. Health First: Following the principles in Chapter 2.1, Raj created a morning routine that started with 30 minutes of yoga and proper nutrition. Within three months, he lost 15kg and his energy levels stabilized.

2. Relationship Rebuilding: Using the techniques from Chapter 4.2, he scheduled weekly non-negotiable time with his parents and reached out to reconnect with old friends who shared his values.

3. Purpose Discovery: Through the exercises in Chapter 5.1, Raj realized his passion for teaching and mentoring. He started volunteering to train junior developers at weekend workshops.

4. Wealth Rebalancing: While maintaining his career, Raj applied the principles from Chapter 3.3 to create boundaries at work and developed a financial plan that would eventually allow him to transition to teaching full-time.

"The Four Pillars approach completely changed my perspective. I realized success isn't just about career achievement or money—it's about creating harmony across all areas of life. The most surprising thing was that when I focused on health, relationships, and purpose, my work performance actually improved because I was happier and more energized."

Where Is Raj Now?

Three years after his transformation began, Raj has maintained his health improvements and has regular family dinners twice a week. He negotiated a 4-day work week with his company and uses his fifth day to run a coding academy for underprivileged children. His savings plan is on track for him to transition to teaching full-time within two years.

"I'm earning slightly less than before, but my quality of life has improved tenfold. I no longer measure success by my salary but by whether I'm thriving in all four pillars of my life."

Reflection Questions:

1. Like Raj, are there areas of your life you've been neglecting while focusing on just one pillar? Which ones?

2. What would your own Four Pillars Audit reveal about the balance in your life right now?

3. What "turning point moment" might be trying to get your attention that you've been ignoring?

Action Steps:

1. Complete your own Four Pillars Audit (from Chapter 1.4)

2. Identify one small action you can take in your most neglected pillar this week

3. Schedule a "life review" session every month to assess your balance across all four pillars

Sarah's Story: From Financial Anxiety to Freedom

Wealth HealthP urpose

Sarah, a 41-year-old single mother of two from London, had spent most of her adult life living paycheck to paycheck. Despite having a stable job as an administrative assistant, she was drowning in credit card debt and felt constant anxiety about money.

"I would lie awake at night worrying about how I would pay for my children's education or what would happen if I lost my job," Sarah shares. "The stress affected my health—I had chronic headaches, stress-induced eczema, and was emotionally exhausted all the time."

Sarah's financial situation seemed impossible to escape. Her salary barely covered her basic expenses, and each unexpected cost pushed her further into debt. The thought of creating wealth or financial freedom seemed like a fantasy reserved for others.

Turning Point Moment:

"My daughter asked if she could join a school trip abroad, and I had to say no because I couldn't afford it. The look of disappointment on her face broke my heart. That night, I realized I needed to break the cycle—not just for me, but for my children. I didn't want them to inherit my money fears and limitations."

Sarah began her transformation with the Money Mindset principles from Chapter 3.1. She realized her belief that "money is always scarce" and "wealth is for other people" had been programming her financial decisions for decades.

Steps Sarah Took to Transform Her Financial Life:

1. **Mindset Reset:** Using the techniques in Chapter 3.1, Sarah began challenging her limiting beliefs about money and replacing them with empowering alternatives.

2. **Financial Education:** She dedicated 30 minutes each evening to learning about personal finance through free online resources.

3. **Smart Budgeting:** Implementing the 50/30/20 rule from Chapter 3.3, Sarah created her first proper budget and found small expenses she could cut without affecting quality of life.

4. **Side Hustle Development:** Following the framework in Chapter 3.4, Sarah identified her administrative skills could be valuable as a virtual assistant. She started offering her services on weekends.

5. **Debt Strategy:** Rather than just making minimum payments, she used the debt snowball method to systematically eliminate her credit cards one by one.

"The most powerful change wasn't in my bank account—it was in my head. When I stopped thinking like a financially struggling person and started thinking like someone who could create wealth, opportunities I never noticed before suddenly became visible. My side hustle now earns me more than my day job, and I'm teaching my children healthy money habits I wish I'd learned earlier."

Where Is Sarah Now?

Two years after beginning her financial transformation, Sarah has paid off all her credit card debt and built an emergency fund for the first time in her life. Her virtual assistant business has grown to the point where she's considering transitioning to it full-time. Most importantly, her stress-related health issues have diminished, and she's been able to say "yes" to her children's educational opportunities.

"I recently took my children on their first overseas holiday—something I never thought would be possible. When my daughter thanked me for 'becoming different about money,' I knew all the hard work had been worth it."

Reflection Questions:

1. What limiting beliefs about money might be holding you back from financial progress?

2. How has your financial situation affected other pillars of your life (health, relationships, purpose)?

3. What skills or knowledge do you already possess that could potentially generate additional income?

Action Steps:

1. Write down your three strongest limiting beliefs about money and create alternative empowering beliefs

2. Create your first budget using the 50/30/20 rule from Chapter 3.3

3. List three potential side hustle ideas based on your current skills and interests

Miguel's Story: From Disconnection to Deep Relationships

Relationships Purpose Health

At 36, Miguel had built a successful career as a management consultant in Madrid. He'd prioritized professional achievement above all else, moving cities frequently for career advancement and working long hours. While his professional network was extensive, his personal relationships were shallow and transactional.

"I had 500+ LinkedIn connections but no one I could call at 2 AM if I needed help," Miguel explains. "I'd missed family weddings, lost touch with childhood friends, and had a string of short-term romantic relationships that never developed depth. I lived alone in a beautiful apartment that felt empty most of the time."

Despite outward success, Miguel struggled with loneliness and a growing sense that something fundamental was missing from his life. His mental health began deteriorating with symptoms of depression, and he found himself using work as an escape from the emptiness he felt.

Turning Point Moment:

"I was hospitalized with pneumonia, and it took three days before anyone from my personal life noticed I was missing. My secretary eventually called a cousin when I didn't show up for meetings. I realized that if I died, my eulogy would be full of professional achievements but empty of meaningful human connections. That terrified me."

After recovering, Miguel used the Inner Circle assessment from Chapter 4.1 and was shocked to discover he couldn't identify five people who genuinely cared about his wellbeing beyond his professional value.

Steps Miguel Took to Transform His Relationships:

1. Relationship Audit: Using tools from Chapter 4.1, Miguel categorized his existing relationships and identified where he needed deeper connections.

2. Vulnerability Practice: Following exercises from Chapter 4.2, he began practicing authentic communication, starting with reconnecting with family members.

3. Boundary Setting: Implementing strategies from Chapter 4.3, Miguel established work-life boundaries for the first time, including no-work weekends.

4. Community Building: He joined a local hiking club and a language exchange group to meet people with shared interests outside of work.

5. Digital Detox: Miguel created technology-free zones in his life to encourage deeper presence in his interactions.

"I had to learn that relationships aren't efficient—they're messy, time-consuming, and don't follow project timelines. But they're also the most rewarding investment I've ever made. I've learned that vulnerability isn't weakness; it's the only path to authentic connection. My relationships now give me a sense of belonging I never knew I was missing."

Where Is Miguel Now?

Eighteen months after his relationship transformation began, Miguel has rebuilt connections with family and established close friendships through his new community activities. He's in a committed romantic relationship for the first time in a decade and has restructured his work to allow more time for relationships. His symptoms of depression have significantly decreased, and he reports feeling "at home in the world" for the first time in his adult life.

"I still value my career, but it's no longer the center of my identity. I've learned that no professional achievement can replace the feeling of being truly known and accepted by others."

Reflection Questions:

1. Who are the five people you could call in a genuine emergency at any hour? If you struggle to name five, what might that indicate?

2. In what ways might you be using work or other activities to avoid the vulnerability of deep relationships?

3. What boundaries might you need to establish to create space for meaningful connections in your life?

Action Steps:

1. Complete the Inner Circle assessment from Chapter 4.1

2. Identify one relationship you'd like to deepen and take a concrete step this week (e.g., schedule a meaningful conversation, not just a casual meetup)

3. Establish one new boundary to protect time for relationships (e.g., no work emails after 7 PM)

Aisha's Story: From Aimless Career to Purposeful Calling

Purpose Wealth Relationships

Aisha, a 29-year-old marketing manager from Dubai, had followed the traditional path to success. Good grades, prestigious university, corporate job with regular promotions. By external measures, she was thriving. Internally, however, she felt increasingly disconnected from her work.

"I was good at my job and it paid well, but it felt meaningless," Aisha recalls. "I dreaded Monday mornings and lived for the weekends. My creativity was dying, and I started to feel like I was just a cog in a machine, helping sell products nobody really needed."

The gap between her external success and internal emptiness created growing anxiety. Aisha found herself wondering if something was wrong with her for not being satisfied with what others considered a dream career.

Turning Point Moment:

"During a performance review, my manager asked where I saw myself in five years. The question triggered a minor panic attack because I suddenly realized I couldn't bear the thought of doing this work for five more years. When I couldn't answer, he suggested a director-level promotion path, and I nodded while thinking, 'This would make me miserable.' I knew then something had to change."

Aisha began her transformation by using the Ikigai framework from Chapter 5.1 to explore the intersection of what she loved, what she was good at, what the world needed, and what she could be paid for.

Steps Aisha Took to Find Her Purpose:

1.   Purpose Discovery: Using the exercises from Chapter 5.1, Aisha identified that her passion for storytelling, community building, and cultural preservation were core to her sense of purpose.

2.   Skill Inventory: Following the framework in Chapter 5.3, she cataloged her transferable skills from marketing that could apply to more meaningful work.

3. Side Project Testing: Implementing the passion-testing approach from Chapter 5.4, Aisha started documenting traditional recipes and stories from elderly community members as a weekend project.

4. Network Reimagining: Using strategies from Chapter 4.1, she began connecting with people working in cultural preservation and digital storytelling.

5. Financial Preparation: Applying principles from Chapter 3.3, she created a financial runway that would allow her to eventually transition careers safely.

"Finding my purpose wasn't about discovering something new—it was about reconnecting with what had always been meaningful to me but that I'd ignored to follow a conventional path. The most powerful question I asked myself was: 'What work would I do even if I wasn't paid for it?' Once I answered that honestly, the path became clear."

Where Is Aisha Now?

Two years after her turning point, Aisha has transitioned to working as a digital content creator focused on preserving and sharing cultural heritage. Her documentary series on traditional cooking techniques has gained international recognition. She earns less than her corporate role initially, but her work feels significant and meaningful. Most importantly, she now jumps out of bed on Monday mornings excited to begin her week.

"I've realized that purpose isn't just about what you do—it's about why you do it and who you serve. My skills haven't changed dramatically, but the context and intention have transformed completely."

Reflection Questions:

1. What activities make you lose track of time when you're engaged in them?

2. If money were no object, what work would you choose to do?

3. What have you always been naturally good at that you might be undervaluing?

Key Lessons from These Transformation Stories

These four stories demonstrate several important principles about personal transformation:

1. Transformation often begins with crisis. For most people, significant change doesn't happen when things are comfortable. It takes a turning point—sometimes painful—to create the motivation for real change.

2. The Four Pillars are interconnected. Notice how each person's story shows how improvement in one area positively impacted other areas. Raj's health improvements boosted his work performance. Sarah's financial transformation improved her health and family relationships. Miguel's relationship focus enhanced his mental health. Aisha's purpose discovery led to better relationships and eventually sustainable income.

3. Small, consistent actions compound over time. None of these transformations happened overnight. They were the result of systematic, persistent steps taken consistently over months and years.

4. Mindset shifts precede external changes. In each case, the person had to change their beliefs and thought patterns before their external reality could transform.

5. Frameworks and systems accelerate progress. Each person used specific tools and methodologies from this book to guide their transformation, rather than relying on willpower or vague aspirations.

As we move into stories of entrepreneurs and leaders in the next section, keep these principles in mind. The scale and context may differ, but the fundamental patterns of transformation remain consistent.

7.2 Lessons from Entrepreneurs, Creators & Leaders

While the previous stories focused on personal transformation, this section explores individuals who've built something significant beyond themselves. These entrepreneurs, creators, and leaders demonstrate how the principles in this book apply to building businesses, creative projects, and movements that impact others.

David's Story: From Corporate Dropout to Social Entrepreneur

Purpose Wealth Relationships

David had spent fifteen years climbing the corporate ladder at a global financial services company. By age 42, he'd reached a senior VP position with a substantial salary, but felt increasingly troubled by the disconnect between his work and his values.

"I was helping wealthy clients become wealthier while seeing so many financial literacy issues in my own community," David explains. "I grew up in a lower-income neighborhood where many families struggled with predatory lending and debt cycles. The contrast between my day job and the reality for most people became too stark to ignore."

Turning Point Moment:

"My mother called me about a cousin who'd fallen into a payday loan trap after a medical emergency. Despite my financial expertise, I realized I'd never used it to help the people who needed it most. That night, I sketched the first outline of what would become my social enterprise on the back of a napkin at my kitchen table."

David began researching social entrepreneurship models that could provide financial education and affordable financial services to underserved communities. Using the Side Hustle framework from Chapter 3.4 and the Purpose-Driven Career Plan from Chapter 5.5, he created a 12-month transition strategy.

How David Built His Social Enterprise:

1. Market Research: David spent weekends conducting community interviews to understand specific financial challenges facing low-income families.

2. Skill Leveraging: Using the Skill Mastery concepts from Chapter 5.3, he identified which of his corporate finance skills could transfer to his social enterprise.

3. Network Transformation: Following principles from Chapter 4.2, David built new relationships with community leaders, non-profit organizations, and impact investors.

4. Minimum Viable Product: He started with weekend financial literacy workshops while still employed, testing his concept with minimal risk.

5. Financial Runway: Using strategies from Chapter 3.3, David created an 18-month savings buffer before leaving his corporate role.

"The transition was terrifying at times. I gave up certainty, status, and a significant portion of my income. But the fear was outweighed by the sense of alignment I finally felt between my daily work and my deepest values. Building something meaningful from scratch has been the most challenging and rewarding experience of my life."

Where Is David Now?

Five years after his turning point, David's social enterprise serves over 15,000 families annually with financial education programs and affordable financial products. The organization employs 23 people, many hired from the communities they serve. While David's income is lower than his corporate salary, his organization has secured sustainable funding through a combination of grants, earned income, and impact investments.

"Success for me now means seeing families break generational cycles of financial struggle. Every time a client starts their first savings account or becomes a first-generation homeowner, I know I'm exactly where I'm meant to be."

Key Entrepreneurial Lessons from David's Journey:

• Purpose-driven businesses solve real problems. David's success came from addressing a genuine need he deeply understood.

• Test before you leap. By starting with weekend workshops, David validated his concept while maintaining financial security.

• Leverage existing skills in new contexts. David's corporate finance background became an asset when repurposed for social impact.

• Build the right relationships. His network transformation was crucial for accessing resources and reaching his target community.

• Financial preparation enables bigger risks. Having an 18-month runway gave David the security to fully commit to his vision.

Lin's Story: From Burnout Creator to Sustainable Success

Health Wealth Purpose

Lin had built a substantial following as a content creator in the wellness space, with over 500,000 followers across social platforms. From the outside, her life looked idyllic—beautiful content, brand partnerships, and a growing online business. Behind the scenes, however, she was burning out rapidly.

"I was working 80+ hours a week, constantly creating content, responding to messages, and managing my team," Lin shares. "The irony wasn't lost on me—I was teaching wellness while my own health was collapsing. I had chronic insomnia, anxiety attacks, and hadn't taken a day off in over a year."

Despite financial success, Lin found herself trapped in a content creation hamster wheel, afraid that taking any break would cause her audience and income to disappear.

Turning Point Moment:

"I was filming a video about stress management when I had a panic attack on camera. Instead of deleting it, something compelled me to edit it

278

minimally and post it with an honest caption about my struggles. The response was overwhelming—thousands of heartfelt comments from followers facing similar challenges. That vulnerability showed me a new path forward."

This moment of authenticity led Lin to reevaluate her entire business model. Using the principles from Chapter 2 on health and Chapter 6 on daily systems, she began restructuring her work to support her wellbeing while still serving her audience.

How Lin Transformed Her Creative Business:

1. Content Batching: Using productivity principles from Chapter 6.3, Lin implemented strict content batching sessions instead of constant creation.

2. Business Model Shift: Following passive income strategies from Chapter 3.5, she pivoted from constant new content to more sustainable digital products.

3. Health Boundaries: Implementing the techniques from Chapter 2.4, Lin established non-negotiable health practices and tech-free time blocks.

4. Team Delegation: She built systems that allowed her team to handle more aspects of the business without her direct involvement.

5. Authentic Messaging: Lin shifted her brand to emphasize "real wellness" that acknowledged struggles rather than portraying perfection.

"I had to confront the uncomfortable truth that I'd built a business that was completely dependent on my constant energy output. The breakthrough came when I realized my audience wasn't just following me for perfect content—they were looking for authentic guidance on their own wellness journeys, including the messy parts. This allowed me to create a more honest relationship with my community while building more sustainable systems."

Where Is Lin Now?

Three years after her transformation began, Lin has successfully restructured her business. She now works 25-30 hours per week while generating more revenue than before through evergreen courses, a membership program, and more strategic brand partnerships. Her content schedule is manageable, and she takes regular periods completely offline. Most importantly, her own health has stabilized with regular sleep, decreased anxiety, and energy for personal relationships.

"My business now serves my life, not the other way around. My content is actually better because it comes from a place of genuine wellbeing rather than depletion. And my audience has grown precisely because I'm more authentic about wellness as a journey rather than a destination."

Key Creator Lessons from Lin's Journey:

• Authenticity builds stronger audience connections than perfection. Lin's most powerful content came from sharing her real struggles.

• Sustainable systems outperform hustle in the long run. By creating more intentional systems, Lin increased both impact and income while working less.

• Health is the foundation for creative success. When Lin prioritized her wellbeing, her creative output actually improved in quality.

• Business models should serve life goals, not vice versa. Restructuring her revenue streams allowed Lin to align her work with her desired lifestyle.

• Vulnerability can be a business strength. What felt risky—sharing her struggles—actually deepened her connection with her audience.

Marcus's Story: From Reluctant Manager to Transformational Leader

Relationships Purpose Health

Marcus was a brilliant individual contributor at a mid-sized technology company who was promoted to lead a team of 12 engineers based on his technical expertise. The transition to management was rocky from the start.

"I had no idea how to lead people," Marcus admits. "I was uncomfortable with confrontation, avoided difficult conversations, and tried to solve all problems myself rather than delegating. Team morale was dropping, deadlines were being missed, and I was working longer hours than ever while growing increasingly resentful."

Six months into his role, Marcus received feedback that his team was dysfunctional and considering leaving. The company offered him leadership coaching as a last resort before considering a change in management.

Turning Point Moment:

"My coach asked me a simple question: 'Do you actually want to be a leader?' I started to give the expected answer about career advancement, but then stopped. The truth was, I didn't know. I'd never considered whether leadership aligned with my strengths or purpose. That question forced me to decide if I wanted to develop as a leader or return to individual contribution."

After reflection, Marcus realized he did want to grow as a leader, but needed to completely transform his approach. Using relationship principles from Chapter 4 and purpose concepts from Chapter 5, he embarked on a leadership development journey.

How Marcus Transformed as a Leader:

1. Purpose Clarification: Using the frameworks from Chapter 5.1, Marcus identified that helping others grow aligned with his deeper values.

2. Relationship Focus: Implementing techniques from Chapter 4.2, he began having regular one-on-ones focused on genuine connection with team members.

3. Emotional Intelligence: Following principles from Chapter 2.2, Marcus worked on developing self-awareness and empathy.

4. Delegation Systems: He created clear processes for distributing work based on team members' strengths rather than trying to do everything himself.

5. Feedback Culture: Marcus established regular, honest feedback in both directions, creating psychological safety for team members to speak up.

"The breakthrough came when I stopped seeing leadership as a technical challenge to solve and started seeing it as a relationship opportunity. My job wasn't to be the smartest person in the room—it was to create conditions where everyone could contribute their best work. Once I shifted from trying to prove my worth through control to enabling others' success, everything changed."

Where Is Marcus Now?

Four years after his leadership transformation began, Marcus now leads a division of 75 people. Employee satisfaction scores for his teams are consistently the highest in the company, and his division has become known for both innovation and psychological safety. Marcus has been recognized with leadership awards and now mentors new managers throughout the organization. Most importantly, he reports finding deeper purpose and satisfaction in developing others than he ever experienced as an individual contributor.

"I now measure my success by the growth of my team members. When someone I've mentored gets promoted or accomplishes something significant, that brings me more fulfillment than any personal achievement."

Key Leadership Lessons from Marcus's Journey:

• Technical expertise doesn't equal leadership ability. Marcus had to develop an entirely new skillset focused on people, not just problems.

• Leadership is fundamentally about relationships. His breakthrough came from focusing on connection rather than control.

• Vulnerability strengthens leadership. When Marcus admitted what he didn't know, it created space for authentic growth.

• Purpose clarity transforms management approach. Understanding his deeper motivation for leading changed how Marcus approached his role.

• Self-awareness precedes team development. Marcus had to grow his emotional intelligence before he could effectively lead others.

Elena's Story: From Idea to Impact

Purpose Wealth Relationships Health

Elena was a 31-year-old environmental scientist who had spent years researching sustainable materials. She had developed a biodegradable alternative to single-use plastics in her lab, but felt frustrated that her innovation remained academic rather than creating real-world impact.

"I was publishing papers that only other scientists read while watching plastic pollution continue to devastate ecosystems," Elena recalls. "I had this solution that could help, but no idea how to bring it out of the lab and into the world."

With no business background and limited resources, Elena faced seemingly insurmountable barriers to commercializing her innovation. The gap between scientific research and market implementation felt impossible to bridge alone.

Turning Point Moment:

"I was at a beach cleanup event when a young girl asked me what happens to all the plastic we were collecting. When I explained that most would still end up in landfills or be incinerated, she asked, 'Then why are we even doing this?' Her innocent question hit me hard. I realized that without systemic solutions, we were just treating symptoms. That day, I decided my research needed to become a product people could actually use."

Elena began exploring how to transform her research into a business. Using principles from Chapters 3, 4, and 5, she methodically built a plan to bring her sustainable material to market.

How Elena Built Her Impact Business:

1.   Purpose Alignment: Using the Ikigai framework from Chapter 5.1, Elena confirmed that commercializing her research aligned perfectly with her purpose.

2.   Skill Gap Analysis: Following the Skill Mastery approach from Chapter 5.3, she identified business areas where she needed development or partners.

3.   Strategic Relationships: Implementing networking strategies from Chapter 4.2, Elena connected with business mentors, manufacturers, and potential investors.

4.   Prototype Development: She created simple product prototypes to demonstrate real-world applications of her material.

5.   Health Balance: Using techniques from Chapter 2, Elena maintained her wellbeing while navigating the startup journey.

"The most challenging part was shifting my identity from 'scientist' to 'entrepreneur.' I had to step outside the comfort zone of research and learn an entirely new set of skills. What kept me going was knowing the environmental impact each successful product would have. Every time I doubted myself, I remembered that girl on the beach and recommitted to creating change at scale."

Where Is Elena Now?

Three years after her turning point, Elena has successfully launched a company that produces biodegradable food packaging from her patented material. The business has secured significant investment, partners with several national food brands, and continues to expand its product line. While still involved in research and development, Elena has assembled a strong team that complements her scientific expertise with business acumen. The company has already prevented over 15 million plastic items from entering the waste stream.

"I still consider myself a scientist at heart, but now I'm a scientist making a tangible difference. The skills I've developed in building this company have been as valuable as my technical knowledge—they've been the bridge between knowing the solution and implementing it at scale."

Key Impact Lessons from Elena's Journey:

• Purpose-driven innovation finds support. Elena's clear environmental mission helped attract partners and resources.

• Knowledge alone doesn't create change. She had to build implementation skills to turn research into real-world impact.

• Strategic relationships accelerate impact. Building the right team and partnerships was crucial for bringing her innovation to market.

• Identity evolution enables growth. Elena had to expand her self-concept from scientist to entrepreneur-scientist.

• Balance sustains long-term impact. By maintaining her health during the startup journey, Elena created sustainable change rather than burning out.

Key Entrepreneurial & Leadership Principles

The stories of David, Lin, Marcus, and Elena reveal several consistent principles for creating impact beyond personal transformation:

1.   Purpose alignment creates resilience. Each person faced significant challenges but persisted because their work aligned deeply with their values and sense of purpose.

2.   Relationships are the foundation of impact. None of these individuals succeeded alone. Their ability to build authentic relationships—with team members, customers, investors, or partners—was crucial for their success.

3.   Personal wellbeing enables sustainable leadership. Those who maintained their health created sustainable ventures, while those who initially neglected it (like Lin) had to restructure to prevent collapse.

4.   Evolving identity precedes external growth. Each person had to expand or shift their identity before they could create their impact. David from financial executive to social entrepreneur. Lin from content creator to business owner. Marcus from technical expert to people leader. Elena from academic researcher to innovation entrepreneur.

5.   Strategic skill development bridges vision and implementation. Each person identified skill gaps and systematically developed or partnered to fill them, turning their vision into reality.

As you consider your own leadership journey or entrepreneurial aspirations, reflect on which of these principles resonates most strongly with your current situation. The path from idea to impact is rarely linear, but these common themes can guide your approach.

Applying These Lessons to Your Leadership Journey

Whether you're currently leading a team, building a business, or simply wanting to have greater impact in your sphere of influence, the stories in this section offer valuable guidance. Here are practical ways to apply these lessons:

For Aspiring Entrepreneurs:

• Start with purpose clarity. Use the Ikigai framework from Chapter 5.1 to ensure your business concept aligns with your deeper purpose.

• Test assumptions affordably. Follow David's approach of starting with minimal-resource weekend projects before making major commitments.

• Build parallel skills while employed. Like Elena, develop necessary business skills alongside your current role before making the leap.

• Create financial runways. Use the principles from Chapter 3.3 to build savings that can sustain you through the early stages of entrepreneurship.

• Design for sustainability from day one. Learn from Lin's story by creating business models that don't rely on your constant energy expenditure.

For Current or Aspiring Leaders:

• Clarify your leadership purpose. Like Marcus, reflect on whether leadership truly aligns with your values and strengths.

• Prioritize relationship development. Invest time in genuine connection with team members rather than focusing exclusively on tasks.

• Build self-awareness. Use the emotional intelligence practices from Chapter 2.2 to recognize your triggers and patterns.

• Create psychological safety. Establish environments where team members can speak honestly and take appropriate risks.

• Measure success through others' growth. Shift your definition of achievement from personal accomplishment to team development.

For Impact-Focused Individuals:

• Identify leverage points. Like Elena, look for opportunities where your specific knowledge or skills could create systemic change.

• Bridge knowledge and action. Develop implementation capabilities that translate your ideas into real-world impact.

• Build strategic alliances. Identify partners whose strengths complement yours to expand your potential impact.

• Start where you are. Each story demonstrates that impact begins with using existing resources and knowledge in new ways.

• Maintain personal wellbeing. Sustainable impact requires sustainable personal practices.

7.3 Your Success Journal

Now that you've explored real stories of transformation and impact, it's time to reflect on your own journey. This Success Journal section provides a structured framework for applying the lessons from this book to your specific circumstances.

Taking time for reflection is not a luxury—it's an essential practice for growth. As the ancient philosopher Socrates observed, "The unexamined life is not worth living." This journal will help you examine your life across the four pillars and create a personalized path forward.

Part 1: Assessing Your Current Reality

Before you can create a plan for transformation, you need to accurately understand your starting point. These reflection exercises will help you assess where you currently stand in each of the four life pillars.

Health Assessment

On a scale of 1-10, how would you rate your current:

- Physical energy levels: ______

- Quality of sleep: ______

- Nutrition habits: ______

- Exercise consistency: ______

- Mental clarity: ______

- Emotional stability: ______

- Stress management: ______

What are your biggest health strengths right now?

____

____

____

What are your most significant health challenges?

____

____

Wealth Assessment

On a scale of 1-10, how would you rate your current:

- Income satisfaction: _______

- Savings habits: _______

- Debt management: _______

- Financial knowledge: _______

- Financial security: _______

- Income diversity: _______

- Money mindset: _______

What are your biggest financial strengths right now?

____

____

What are your most significant financial challenges?

____

____

Relationships Assessment

On a scale of 1-10, how would you rate your current:

- Close friendship quality: _______

- Family relationships: _______

- Romantic relationship (if applicable): _______

- Professional relationships: _______

- Social support network: _______

- Communication skills: _______

- Boundary maintenance: _______

Who are the five most important people in your life right now?

____

____

What relationship areas need the most attention?

____

____

Purpose Assessment

On a scale of 1-10, how would you rate your current:

- Career fulfillment: _______

- Alignment with values: _______

- Use of strengths: _______

- Growth opportunities: _______

- Impact on others: _______

- Daily meaning: _______

- Future clarity: _______

What activities currently give you the greatest sense of purpose?

____

____

____

____

____

____

What aspects of your work or life feel misaligned with your deeper purpose?

____

____

____

Part 2: Identifying Your Transformation Priorities

Based on your assessments, identify which areas need the most attention right now. Remember that you don't need to transform everything simultaneously. Strategic focus on one or two areas often creates positive ripple effects across all pillars.

Priority Identification

Which life pillar currently needs the most attention? (Circle one)

Health | Wealth | Relationships | Purpose

Within this pillar, what specific aspect would create the greatest positive impact if improved?

____

____

____

Why is this important to you? Connect this to your deeper values and goals.

____

____

____

Support Pillar

Which secondary pillar would best support your primary focus area? (Circle one)

Health | Wealth | Relationships | Purpose

How might improvements in this support pillar help you succeed in your primary focus area?

____

____

____

____

Your Transformation Story

Which case study from this chapter resonates most with your current situation? Why?

____

____

____

What specific strategies from that person's journey could you adapt for your situation?

____

____

____

Part 3: Creating Your 90-Day Transformation Plan

Now that you've identified your priorities, it's time to create a concrete plan. The 90-day timeframe provides enough time for meaningful change while maintaining focus and urgency.

Your 90-Day Vision

Describe in detail how your life will be different in 90 days if you successfully focus on your priority areas. Be specific about what will have changed.

____

____

____

____

____

____

____

____

____

____

Key Milestones

Break down your 90-day journey into three 30-day milestone targets:

First 30 Days Target:

____

____

____

60-Day Milestone:

____

____

____

90-Day Achievement:

____

____

____

Weekly Action Commitments

What specific actions will you commit to each week? (Be realistic and specific)

Weekly Health Actions:

____

____

____

Weekly Wealth Actions:

____

____

____

Weekly Relationship Actions:

____

____

Weekly Purpose Actions:

____

____

____

Part 4: Anticipating and Overcoming Obstacles

Every transformation journey faces challenges. Anticipating potential obstacles and preparing strategies to overcome them dramatically increases your chances of success.

Obstacle Planning

What are the three biggest obstacles you're likely to face during your 90-day transformation?

Obstacle 1:

____

____

Strategy to overcome:

____

____

Obstacle 2:

____

____

Strategy to overcome:

____

____

Obstacle 3:

____

____

Strategy to overcome:

____

____

Support System

Who can support you during this transformation journey? (Name specific people)

____

____

____

How specifically will you ask for their support?

____

____

____

____

Part 5: Daily Success Habits

Transformation happens through consistent daily actions. This section helps you identify and commit to the daily habits that will move you toward your goals.

Morning Routine Design

Based on Chapter 6.1, design your ideal morning routine:

____

____

____

____

Evening Review Practice

Design a simple evening review practice to maintain awareness of your progress:

____

____

____

____

Weekly Planning Commitment

When specifically will you conduct your weekly planning session? (Day and time)

____

____

What will you review during this weekly session?

____

____

Part 6: Tracking Your Transformation

As Chapter 6.3 emphasizes, tracking your progress is essential for maintaining momentum and making adjustments. This section provides templates for monitoring your transformation journey.

Weekly Tracking Template

Date: _______________ to _______________

Priority Pillar Progress (Scale 1-10): ______

Key Wins This Week:

____
____
____
____
____

Challenges Faced:

____
____

Lessons Learned:

____
____

Adjustments Needed:

____
____

Focus for Next Week:

____
____

Monthly Review Template

Month: _______________

Progress in Health Pillar (1-10): ______

Progress in Wealth Pillar (1-10): ______

Progress in Relationships Pillar (1-10): ______

Progress in Purpose Pillar (1-10): ______

Most Significant Change This Month:

____

____

____

Habits That Are Working Well:

____

____

____

Habits That Need Adjustment:

____

____

Focus For Next Month:

____

____

Part 7: Celebrating Progress

Acknowledging and celebrating your growth is crucial for maintaining motivation. This section helps you recognize your progress and use it to fuel further transformation.

Progress Celebration Plan

How will you celebrate achieving your 30-day milestone?

____

____

How will you celebrate achieving your 60-day milestone?

____

____

How will you celebrate achieving your 90-day milestone?

____

____

Transformation Evidence Journal

Use this space to document evidence of your transformation as it occurs—changes others notice, moments of breakthrough, new opportunities that emerge, etc.

____

____

____

____

____

____

____

____

____

____

____

Part 8: Your Future Self Vision

Looking beyond your 90-day plan, this section helps you envision your longer-term transformation and the person you're becoming.

One-Year Vision

One year from today, how will your life be different if you continue this transformation journey? Be specific about changes in each pillar.

Health:

____

____

Wealth:

____

____

Relationships:

____

____

Purpose:

____

____

Letter From Your Future Self

Write a letter from your future self one year from now, looking back on the transformation journey you're beginning today. What would your future self want to tell you about this path?

____

____

____

____

____

____

Your Commitment Contract

To solidify your transformation plan, create a formal commitment to yourself. This contract makes your intentions explicit and increases your likelihood of following through.

Personal Transformation Commitment

I, ______________________________, commit to my 90-day transformation journey beginning on _______________ (date).

My primary focus will be improving my _______________ pillar, specifically by

____

____

I understand that transformation requires consistent effort, and I commit to the daily and weekly actions outlined in my plan. I will track my progress, celebrate my wins, and adjust my approach when needed.

When obstacles arise, I will not give up but instead use the strategies I've identified to overcome them. I will draw support from my community and the principles in this book.

I make this commitment because

____

____

____

_______________________________.

Signature: _________________________________

Date: _________________________________

Witness (optional): _________________________

As you complete this Success Journal section, remember that transformation is not a one-time event but an ongoing process. The journal templates provided here can be used repeatedly as you continue to grow and evolve across all four life pillars.

Your journey of breaking free from feeling stuck has truly begun. In our final section, we'll explore some concluding thoughts on maintaining your transformation momentum for the long term.

Conclusion

As we come to the end of this book, let's reflect on the journey we've taken together and look ahead to what comes next for you.

The Four Pillars Revisited

Throughout this book, we've explored the four fundamental pillars that form the foundation of a fulfilled, successful life:

Health – We discovered that physical energy, mental clarity, and emotional resilience are not luxuries but necessities for sustainable success. Your health practices—from morning routines to stress management—create the energy that powers everything else in your life. Remember that your body is the vehicle through which you experience every moment of your life. Caring for it is not selfish; it's essential.

Wealth – We explored how financial freedom comes not just from earning more but from transforming your relationship with money. By building multiple income streams, mastering smart budgeting, and developing passive income sources, you create the economic foundation that supports your choices and opportunities. Money itself is not the goal, but rather the freedom and options it provides.

Relationships – We learned that deep, meaningful connections with others are perhaps the greatest predictor of both happiness and success. Your inner circle shapes your identity, opportunities, and resilience during challenges. By intentionally building authentic relationships and learning to set healthy boundaries, you create a support system that enhances every aspect of life.

Purpose – We discovered that aligning your daily work with your deepest values and natural strengths creates a sense of meaning that transcends conventional success. Whether through career transformation or finding purpose within your current path, connecting to something larger than yourself brings fulfillment that no achievement alone can provide.

As the stories in Part 7 illustrated, these pillars are not separate compartments but interconnected aspects of a whole life. Progress in one area creates positive momentum in others. Similarly, neglect in one pillar eventually undermines the others.

The Transformation Process

Through the experiences shared in this book, we've seen that meaningful transformation follows a consistent pattern:

1. Honest assessment of your current reality across all four pillars

2. Clear vision of what you want to create in each area

3. Strategic focus on your highest-leverage opportunities for growth

4. Consistent systems that translate intentions into daily actions

5. Community support from people who believe in your potential

6. Regular reflection to celebrate progress and adjust approach

7. Persistent resilience when facing inevitable obstacles

This process is not linear but cyclical. As you grow in one area, you'll revisit these steps for new challenges and opportunities. Transformation is not a destination but an ongoing journey of becoming more fully yourself and expressing your unique potential.

Beyond the Book: Continuing Your Journey

While this book provides a comprehensive framework for transformation, your journey is just beginning. Here are suggestions for maintaining your momentum:

• Implement your 90-day plan. The Success Journal section provides everything you need to create immediate change. Don't wait for the "perfect" time—start with one small action today.

• Revisit key chapters. As you encounter specific challenges, return to relevant sections for guidance. This book is designed to be a reference you can use repeatedly.

• Find accountability partners. Share your transformation goals with someone who will support and challenge you. Consider creating a small group that meets regularly to discuss your progress.

• Schedule quarterly reviews. Every three months, assess your progress across all four pillars and set new targets. This regular rhythm keeps your transformation front of mind.

• Teach what you're learning. One of the best ways to integrate new knowledge is to share it with others. As you apply these principles, look for opportunities to mentor those on similar journeys.

Final Thoughts: The Courage to Transform

Transformation requires courage. It means facing uncomfortable truths about where you are now. It means taking risks when outcomes aren't guaranteed. It means persisting through setbacks and disappointments. It means changing deeply ingrained habits and sometimes disappointing others who prefer you to remain the same.

But this courage is accessible to everyone. It's not a special quality reserved for extraordinary people; it's a choice available to anyone willing to take one small step toward change, then another, then another.

The stories shared throughout this book demonstrate that transformation is possible regardless of your starting point. People from diverse backgrounds, facing various challenges, have broken free from feeling stuck and created lives of freedom, purpose, and fulfillment. Their journeys weren't perfect or linear, but they were real. And if they could do it, so can you.

Remember that transformation isn't about becoming someone else—it's about becoming more fully yourself. It's about aligning your daily reality with your deepest values and highest potential. It's about creating a life where all four pillars—health, wealth, relationships, and purpose—support and enhance each other.

As you close this book and begin (or continue) your transformation journey, know that the author and everyone whose stories have been shared here are cheering you on. We believe in your capacity to break free from whatever holds you back and create a life that truly reflects who you are meant to be.

The journey of a thousand miles begins with a single step. Your next step awaits. Take it today.

A Personal Letter from Chandan Bera

Dear Reader,

If you've made it this far, I want to personally thank you for the time and attention you've given to this book. In a world full of distractions, the choice to invest in your growth demonstrates a commitment to yourself that already sets you apart.

While I've shared principles, strategies, and stories throughout these pages, there's one message I want to emphasize above all: You have everything you need to begin your transformation journey right now.

You don't need more information, better circumstances, or special qualifications. You need only the willingness to take one small action today, then another tomorrow. Transformation happens not through grand, dramatic changes but through consistent small choices that compound over time.

I wrote this book because I've experienced both the pain of feeling stuck and the joy of breaking free. I've known the frustration of seeing others succeed while feeling left behind, and I've discovered the principles that bridge that gap. Every strategy in this book has been tested—either in my own life or in the lives of people I've had the privilege to work with.

What I want most is for this book to be not just read but used. My greatest hope is that these pages show signs of wear—highlighted passages, dog-eared corners, margin notes—because that would mean you're engaging actively with these ideas rather than passively consuming them.

As you move forward, remember that setbacks are not failures but feedback. Every person whose story appears in this book faced obstacles, made mistakes, and sometimes lost momentum. What defined their success wasn't perfection but persistence—the willingness to keep going, to learn from experience, and to begin again with greater wisdom.

I believe in you and the unique contribution you have to make in this world. I believe that as you strengthen each of the four pillars in your life, you'll discover capacities within yourself you didn't know existed. And I believe that your transformation will create ripples that positively impact countless others in ways you may never fully see.

If this book has impacted you in any way, I'd be honored to hear your story. Nothing brings me greater fulfillment than knowing these principles are creating real change in real lives.

With gratitude and belief in your journey,

Chandan Bera

Your Journey Begins Now: 7-Day Kickstart Plan

While your Success Journal contains your comprehensive 90-day plan, here's a simple 7-day kickstart to build immediate momentum. Each day focuses on one small action in each pillar that you can complete in 15 minutes or less.

Day 1: Assessment Day

• Health: Take a 10-minute walk while reflecting on your current energy levels.

• Wealth: List all your income sources and fixed expenses.

• Relationships: Identify your five most important relationships.

• Purpose: Write down three activities that make you lose track of time.

Day 2: Foundation Day

• Health: Go to bed 30 minutes earlier than usual.

• Wealth: Set up an automatic transfer of even a small amount to savings.

• Relationships: Send a message of appreciation to someone important to you.

• Purpose: Spend 10 minutes journaling about what makes work meaningful to you.

Day 3: Clarity Day

- Health: Drink water instead of one sugary or caffeinated beverage.

- Wealth: Identify one unnecessary expense you can eliminate.

- Relationships: Schedule a quality time activity with someone you care about.

- **Purpose: List three skills you most enjoy using.**

Day 4: Action Day

- Health: Do a 7-minute high-intensity workout (find free videos online).

- Wealth: Research one potential side income opportunity for 15 minutes.

- Relationships: Have a conversation where you practice listening more than speaking.

- Purpose: Identify one way to bring more meaning into your current work.

Day 5: Mindset Day

- Health: Practice 5 minutes of mindfulness meditation.

- Wealth: Write down your three strongest limiting beliefs about money.

- Relationships: Identify one boundary you need to establish or strengthen.

- Purpose: Consider how your work impacts others positively, even in small ways.

Day 6: Growth Day

- Health: Add one extra serving of vegetables to your day.

- Wealth: Listen to 15 minutes of a financial podcast or audiobook.

- Relationships: Reach out to someone you've lost touch with but value.

• Purpose: Research opportunities to use your skills in service of a cause you care about.

Day 7: Integration Day

• Health: Create a simple morning routine for the coming week.

• Wealth: Schedule a recurring 30-minute money management session your calendar.

• Relationships: Plan a regular connection ritual with someone important to you.

• Purpose: Identify one project that would help you explore your potential purpose more deeply.

• Integration: Reflect on which pillar creates the most positive impact when you focus on it, and make this your priority for week two.

After completing this 7-day kickstart, you'll have established initial momentum in all four pillars and gained clarity about where to focus next. Return to your Success Journal to continue building on this foundation with your comprehensive 90-day plan.

Remember: transformation happens one day, one choice, one action at a time. The journey of breaking free has begun.

About the Author

Chandan Bera is a personal development coach, author, and speaker dedicated to helping people break free from feeling stuck and create lives of freedom, purpose, and fulfillment across all four life pillars.

Drawing from extensive study of both Eastern wisdom traditions and modern success principles, Chandan has developed practical frameworks that have helped thousands of clients transform their health, wealth, relationships, and sense of purpose.

After experiencing his own journey from feeling stuck to finding freedom, Chandan dedicated himself to sharing the principles and practices that create lasting change. His unique approach combines ancient philosophical insights with evidence-based strategies, delivered in accessible, actionable formats.

Chandan's work is guided by the belief that everyone deserves to live a life aligned with their deepest values and highest potential. Through his books, coaching programs, and speaking engagements, he continues to expand his mission of empowering others to break free from limitation and create lives of true success.

"The greatest freedom is being able to fully express who you truly are while creating positive impact in the world."

— **Chandan Bera**